M000224107

A SELF-CARE SYSTEM
FOR PURPOSEFUL LIVING

STACY FISHER-GUNN

Intrinsic Publishing
Issaquah, Washington

UPPWARD

Intrinsic Publishing
Issaquah, Washington

eISBN: 978-0-9974853-1-8

This publication is not intended to replace medical advice, diagnosis, care or treatment.

To learn more about designing your own self-care practice, visit us at:
www.LivingUpp.com

To my husband, Jeremy, for your
love, support and patience

TABLE OF CONTENTS

Preface..i

Introduction..v

What is Self-Care?..vii

How to Use This Book xvii

Chapter 1: Systemic Health 1

    Hydrating 2

    Eating Real Food 4

    Avoiding Nutritional Reductionism.................14

    Moving..24

    Resting 28

    Preventing Chronic Medical Conditions 30

    Managing Chronic Medical Conditions............32

    Balancing 35

Chapter 2: Emotive Health 39

    Communicating 40

    Cultivating Positivity 41

    Being Optimistic 48

    Dealing with Negativity 51

    Finding Meaning 54

Chapter 3: Luminescent Health 57

Being Authentic 59

Cultivating Self-Awareness 61

Changing our Behaviors....................................65

Enjoying the Moment 71

Playing 73

Chapter 4: Financial Health 77

Assessing Needs 78

Defining Enough 81

Spending...85

Budgeting 86

Saving 88

Downsizing 89

Chapter 5: Cognitive Health 93

Visualizing...94

Accepting...95

Meditating 97

Affirming..98

Being Mindful 99

Building Resiliency 100

Letting Go of Expectations 101

Chapter 6: Aptitudinal Health...........................105

Knowing Our Strengths....................................106

Learning...106

Discovering Our Purpose 109

Taking Risks 111

PREFACE

In 2015, I quit my job without having another one to go to. Was it scary? You bet. Irresponsible? Not at all. A year later, I felt more focused and energized than I ever imagined, and I realize now that having time away gave me the space to find clarity of purpose.

Looking back, my heart was the first to sense the restlessness, and by the time the inner whispers had turned into shouting pleas, I was writing my letter of resignation. At that moment, there were only two things I knew for sure: 1) I wanted to experience more positivity and a deeper sense of meaning in my life, and 2) I was ready to stop thinking about it and actually do something about it.

I've always been an avid planner who engineers every detail of my life, so I'm sure the news of my unemployment came as quite a shock to my friends and family. Being without a job certainly wasn't in my career plan. In fact, like most thirty-somethings, I'd spent the past 15 years of my life working long hours, being permanently attached to my phone and computer and looking for opportunities to advance my career. I was proud of my accomplishments, but the truth was I felt restless, and I knew I needed to refocus my energy.

In an attempt to avoid the strange looks I often received from people after explaining how I arrived at being voluntarily unemployed, I began referring to my hiatus as a "sabbatical." (It turns out taking a year-long career break isn't that common outside of academic settings—but I think that's about to change.) Whatever you choose to call it—a sabbatical, an extended leave or a career break—the reality is that I tapped out and redirected my focus back to my core values: my family, my desire to make a significant contribution to the world and my own personal health.

I began to think of my life as a new startup venture—what Eric Ries, author of *The Lean Startup* (2011), defines as creating something "under conditions of extreme uncertainty." Indeed, my future was uncertain at best, but it was also bursting at the seams with potential.

With that same entrepreneurial mindset, during the first week of my sabbatical I started a new company called Living Upp (www.LivingUpp.com). It just sort of happened. The word "upp" was intended initially to be an acronym for *uniting positivity* with *purpose*, but what I discovered along the way was that I wasn't alone in my quest for more meaning. I talked with many others who shared a similar desire to live with a deeper sense of purpose. Since that time, "upp" has matured into a more dynamic description that reflects the company's broader mission: to unite *people* with *positivity, possibilities* and *purpose.* (Perhaps we'll need to add more p's.)

My hope was that taking time off would give me an opportunity to explore some new possibilities that I hadn't had time to consider while juggling a full-time job. (This book is a great example of one!) Additionally, I wanted to develop a sustainable self-care practice that would enable me to make a more meaningful contribution to the world.

The ideas presented in this book are a collection of the experiences and knowledge that I've acquired both personally and professionally, much of which was influenced by other forward thinkers like Martin Seligman, Jean Anthelme Brillat-Savarin, William Miller, Stephen Rollnick, Molly Kellogg, Marion Nestle, Carlo Petrini, Viktor Frankl, Barbara Fredrickson, Bill Mollison, Byron Katie and countless other everyday people that I've encountered over the course of my life. I hope that you find these words encouraging and motivating, and that you choose to take action on your intentions so that you can enjoy the process of bringing them to life.

The most significant thing I've learned throughout this process is that to fully experience my life's purpose, I must be willing to make mistakes, accept criticism, get laughed at, be disappointed and still have the strength to get up and try again. That is what living "upp" is about.

INTRODUCTION

Over the course of my career as a library aide, waitress, factory worker, registered dietitian/nutritionist, business owner, health & wellness coach and leader, I've discovered that self-care is something most people understand as a basic concept, but one that few practice consistently. Life's endless demands have a way of redirecting our attention, often to the extent that we neglect ourselves.

As I eased into my sabbatical, I began to see the value of self-care more clearly. I realized that there were more facets to health than the widely accepted (and perhaps over-simplified) *mind, body and spirit* ideal we have come to recognize in many wellness circles. As a dietitian who was deeply involved in the nutritional aspects of health, I began to realize that such a narrow focus was not consistent with other whole-system philosophies, such as yoga and permaculture. It's clear that the whole of our health is much greater than the sum of its parts, and it's up to each of us to ensure that we are caring for ourselves as a whole.

With that in mind, I developed a unique self-care model that I feel better captures the interconnected complexities of our well-being. The model consists of eight distinct dimensions of self-care: *Systemic, Emotive, Luminescent, Financial, Cognitive, Aptitudinal, Relational* and *Environmental*, along with a unique goal-setting process called *What, Why, How, Do It Now!*

Introduction

Our traditional health care system focuses primarily on the physical aspects of health—our nutritional status, fitness level, laboratory values, organ function, signs and symptoms of disease, as well as our mental and emotional health. The problem with this narrow focus is that it fails to fully encompass the multi-dimensionality of our health. Likewise, many medical providers still use an authoritative approach, expecting patients to "comply" with instructions—because, after all, they know what's best for us. This attitude ignores the fact that we, as patients, are the directors of our own care. We gather information and consider professional input, but ultimately we make the final decision about what, why, how (and whether or not) we will change our behavior.

Self-care helps us cultivate optimal health, which ultimately enables us to live our purpose.

WHAT IS SELF-CARE?

As a new dietitian, I remember reading an interesting article suggesting that Americans are living *shorter* and dying *longer*. I remember considering for the first time that, while we may celebrate increased life expectancies in the U.S., we simultaneously fail to recognize that length of life is not necessarily synonymous with quality of life. And after spending more than 10 years as a consultant in long-term care facilities, I began to understand that much more clearly.

I started to see much younger patients—some barely in their thirties—become permanent residents in nursing homes. Uncontrolled diabetes and other chronic health conditions were robbing them of their freedom to enjoy life. I found myself wishing I had known them earlier in their lives, when they still had a chance to change the direction of their health. While I'm not suggesting all illnesses are directly related to our lifestyle choices, many of them are. For example, we now know that the risk of developing diabetes can be reduced by 58% with lifestyle changes (Diabetes Prevention Program Research Group, 2002). That's pretty significant!

Self-care is about loving and caring for ourselves first, so we can love and care for others more effectively. But it may seem backward to those of us who were brought up believing that sacrificing our own time and comfort is a sign of love. Seen from that perspective, putting ourselves first just seems selfish. (It isn't.)

As one of my fellow book club members once pointed out: there's a reason we're instructed by flight attendants to place the oxygen mask on ourselves before assisting others in the event of an emergency. When we are healthy, we are better equipped to love and serve others.

This book challenges some of those deeply held beliefs by suggesting that regular self-care actually *enhances* our ability to care for others. When we are not burdened by illness, we have the capacity to *do* more, *be* more and *love* more. In the same regard, how we care for ourselves is a reflection of how much we love and value ourselves.

We often neglect self-care because we live in a busy world full of competing priorities, and we've made a habit of sacrificing our own health to please others or to advance our careers. But our short-term successes often come at the expense of our long-term health. With limited resources (in the form of poor health), we are equally limited in our ability to make a contribution.

Furthermore, failing to properly care for ourselves can have an impact on the health of our children. Because they learn by observing us, they begin emulating their role models at a young age. By the time they reach adulthood, their habits are entrenched. A child who has repeatedly seen others sacrificing their own health for the health of others may determine that self-neglect is normal—expected, even.

Self-neglect can stem from many factors. For some, it's purely a knowledge deficit. Many people have never learned how to properly care for themselves to begin with. For others, conflicting health information leaves them feeling paralyzed. As a health coach, I saw this a lot in the form of ambivalence, or indecision. It's pretty hard to set a goal when you can't see the benefits of change.

Another significant benefit of self-care is that it's economical. Health care is expensive when you consider the growing cost of insurance premiums, co-insurance, copays, the cost of medication and treatment and lost time from work. Financial strain causes physical stress, which can lead other health complications. That's why the best strategy is to stay healthy in the first place. And for those who are facing unavoidable health conditions, properly managing them to reduce the risk of progression or complication is also a form of self-care.

Our health is influenced by a number of factors, including personal philosophies, awareness of health risks, sex, gender, age, race, ethnicity, heritage, traditional wisdom, disability, opinions of family and friends, media and advertising messages, beliefs about our own personal constraints and circumstances, personal desires, religion, environmental conditions, genetics, education, social status, cultural norms, government policies, access to health care, financial status, the freedom to choose, and even our spiritual beliefs. Needless to say, many elements play a role in our health decisions.

Health is a state of being that is layered with complexity, and it's easy to see why we prefer to blame external factors than to take personal responsibility. In *High Level Wellness: An Alternative to Doctors, Drugs and Disease,* author Don Ardell (1977) expressed concerns about our culture's displacement of responsibility for our own care. He points out that we neglect our own health and then expect medical professionals to fix us. But this tendency to transfer blame and responsibility for our poor health isn't beneficial. In fact, it only leaves us feeling more helpless. This mindset has caused us to develop an unhealthy dependency on our fragile health care system.

Physicians I have spoken with are equally alarmed. Increasingly, they see patients who are disinterested in self-care, and instead request medication and treatment. Taking ownership of our health, rather than relying on (or blaming) our medical providers, empowers us to become active participants in our lives. We alone have the ability to decide what is right for us, and we alone have the ability to change our habits.

One reason self-neglect is more appealing is that it requires less effort than self-care. Sitting on the couch eating potato chips and watching a movie is a more attractive option to many of us than going to the gym or preparing a healthy meal. But research has shown that people who have the ability to consider the future consequences of their actions (and not give in to short-term pleasures) are more likely to exercise, control their diet, report a lower body mass index (BMI), limit sun exposure and quit smoking (Joireman, 2012). In other words, being able to look beyond the pleasures of today clearly has benefits.

Ironically, we often go to extremes to find ways to live longer, yet we fall prey so easily to near-term desires that shorten our lives. *Blue Zones* author Dan

What is Self-Care?

Buetnner (2012) wrote about the various geographic areas of the world where people live the longest. What do they have in common? Most of them eat plant-based diets, engage in regular physical activity and maintain meaningful connections with others in their community. But Buetnner also points out that aging only has an accelerator pedal. We simply aren't designed to live forever. Our ultimate purpose is to make connections and to help prepare our successors; then move on to the unknown. It's sort of exciting when you think about it.

In some ways, our health care system perpetuates this false notion that immortality is possible. With the right treatment or pill, we are made to believe that our lives will be extended or improved without exerting much effort. It's no surprise, then, why many people are disenchanted with modern medicine, feeling short-changed when a product or treatment fails to deliver the results they expect. All things considered, preventing illness just makes more sense than curing it.

This is why finding a primary care provider that you trust is so important. I have a deep respect for providers who listen to me and present options rather than imposing treatments from a position of authority. I once had an allergist tell me, "I appreciate having well-informed patients, but if you choose not to have the injections, I'm afraid I can no longer see you." (Umm, excuse me?) That comment came after I explained to him that I wanted to take some time to review the handouts he had just given me, and to do some research before I made a decision on treatment. Needless to say, after that response I decided that *I* would no longer see *him*. (Incidentally, I've been getting along just fine without injections.)

But that experience made me wonder how many people get pressured into treatments and medications they don't really want, or don't fully understand. Health care professionals who view patient relationships as partnerships do exist, and they understand their role extends beyond that of simply *providing* care.

The downside to our current health care system's treatment-based approach is that it's built around the idea that we should seek medical care *after* we have a problem. While many providers have shifted to a more modern medical home care delivery model, which also focuses on preventive care, most patients are still limited by what their insurance plans will cover. And that means they may delay treatment or ignore their health needs altogether.

In my private practice as a registered dietitian, this reality was eye-opening for me. I remember receiving a call from a man who explained that he and his family needed help with meal planning. He and his wife had been gaining weight, and more recently he'd noticed that his son was gaining weight too. That's what prompted the call. But after learning that his insurance plan only covered the diagnosis of diabetes he said, "I guess I'll have to call you back when I have a condition my insurance will cover."

Talk about heart-wrenching. I felt helpless. And because of the constraints associated with being a Medicare provider, I wasn't able to adjust my rates. Instead, I began volunteering with Project Access, an organization that provides free medical services and equipment to individuals with financial burdens. Still, the situation troubled me deeply.

Self-care is a powerful tool, especially as we face the uncertainties of health care reform. Change is inevitable, yet there is still significant disagreement about what the ideal model should be. In the meantime, though, we all can do something: be actively involved in our own health.

In some ways, self-care and health care exist on opposite ends of the spectrum. On one end, we have preventive practices (self-care), where we take personal responsibility for our habits, and on the other end we have treatments (health care) that we seek out after we already have a problem, in hopes that someone else will take care of it for us.

It should come as no surprise that preventive care is the simplest and least expensive of the two. By developing a sustainable self-care practice, we can better position ourselves to enjoy good health and have a positive influence on the lives of those we love.

Self-care is about more than just the physical aspects of our health. It's about the entirety of our well-being. The World Health Organization (1946) defines health as "a state of complete physical, mental and social well-being and not merely the absence of disease or infirmity." Good health doesn't just happen; it takes effort.

Our self-care model includes **Eight Dimensions of Self-Care**, which form the mnemonic acronym "SELF-CARE" to make it easy to remember.

SYSTEMIC: How we eat, move and rest
EMOTIVE: How we express ourselves
LUMINESCENT: How we illuminate our inner truth
FINANCIAL: How we allocate our resources
COGNITIVE: How we think
APTITUDINAL: How we contribute to the world
RELATIONAL: How we connect with others
ENVIRONMENTAL: How we harmonize with nature

CHAPTER 1: SYSTEMIC HEALTH

SYSTEMIC: HOW WE EAT, MOVE AND REST

Our systemic health, often referred to as *physical* health, is the most familiar of the eight dimensions because it's the one our health care system focuses on more than any other. We tend to view this dimension as the most important component, but many factors contribute to our overall well-being. Eating, moving and resting are the basic components of this dimensions of self-care, but we'll cover a few others as well.

The primary self-care practices that influence our systemic health are:

Hydrating
Eating Real Food
Avoiding Nutritional Reductionism
Moving
Resting
Preventing Chronic Medical Conditions
Managing Chronic Medical Conditions
Balancing

HYDRATING

With the exception of breathing, water is the most basic human physiological requirement. It's nature's only naturally occurring, non-caloric beverage and it performs a number of vital functions: digestion, transport of nutrients, regulation of body temperature, filtration of wastes, as well as regulation of blood pressure and heart rate. We can only survive for a few days without water, and even mild dehydration has been associated with significant negative health consequences, including impaired cognitive function (Ganio, Armstrong, Casa, et al., 2011). Put simply, water supports life. Most adults are comprised of between 55% and 75% water (Popkin, D'Anci & Rosenberg, 2010).

It may come as a surprise to learn that thirst is not the best indicator of hydration, especially as we age. Even so, you'll be hard-pressed to find a one-size-fits-all recommendation for fluid intake. This is the vague guidance provided on the USDA website:

> "Individual water requirements vary from person to person, and can depend on many factors such as activity level and environment. Most healthy people need to make sure they are drinking enough water, but drinking too much water is usually not an issue" (USDA, 2016).

Similarly, the Institute of Medicine's (IOM) Dietary Reference Intakes (DRI) established an Adequate Intake (AI) level for water, but because this level is based on survey data, the IOM clearly states that it "should not be interpreted as a specific requirement." While it's not a recommendation, per se, the AI for most adult women is 2.7 liters per day (about 11 cups), and for most adult men, 3.7 liters per day (about 15 cups) (USDA, 2016). It's important to note that the AI is based on total water intake, which also includes food sources that can account for 19 to 25% of our daily fluids (Dietary Reference Intakes, 2006).

Some have suggested that six to eight glasses per day is sufficient for most people (though how many ounces in a "glass" is somewhat open to interpretation), while others have popularized the simple 8-by-8 rule: eight 8-oz. glasses per day. Fluid needs vary from individual to individual, which makes establishing a generalized recommendation nearly impossible.

And what about caffeine? The widely accepted notion that caffeine is dehydrating is somewhat of a myth—the research simply doesn't back it up. Habitual caffeine drinkers are less prone to the diuretic effects over time, and even those who are sensitive to caffeine don't suffer from actual dehydration—at least not from natural sources like coffee and tea (Maughan & Griffin, 2003). With that in mind, it's reasonable to believe that caffeinated beverages can actually contribute to our daily fluid intakes after all.

All of that aside, we cannot ignore the fact that some medical conditions (like liver and kidney disease or congestive heart failure) are exacerbated by high amounts of fluid. In some cases, the additional fluid can even be fatal. As cliché as it sounds, talking with your health provider really is the best way to determine your individual fluid needs. (Add that to your list of questions to ask at your next check-up.)

Because hydration is one of the most important aspects of our health, taking time to understand our unique needs is time well spent.

EATING REAL FOOD

Real food (plant- and animal-based foods that are as close to their original state as possible) is the gold standard when it comes to nutrition. But eating real food has become quite challenging. Several years ago I read an article in *Mother Earth News* (2008), in which Joel Salatin said that if we removed all the food in supermarkets that didn't exist before 1900, the shelves would be bare. It's difficult for me to comprehend how our food supply has changed that much in such a relatively short amount of time, but it has changed nonetheless.

Processing, which includes a number of methods for preserving food, is not a new concept. Throughout history, methods like smoking, salt-curing, freezing, fermenting, sun drying, pickling and canning have been used to ensure that food was available throughout the year, especially during times of scarcity, such as through winter or when growing conditions were poor.

Technically speaking, any method used to preserve food is a form of processing.

In recent years, however, "processed" has become synonymous with "unhealthy," and it's easy to see why. Most convenience foods are laden with preservatives and artificial ingredients that leave more questions than answers about their impact on our health.

But if you consider what the definition of "processed" really means, you'd probably agree that not all processed foods are necessarily unhealthy.

Several years ago, I asked a few people with various professional backgrounds what words came to mind when they thought about "processed" foods. Here were some of their responses:

"Altered from its natural state." – Community Relations Director

"Any food that has additives in it." – Teacher

"Food that has been handled, cooked, added to, preservatives added." – Certified Public Accountant

"If it has an ingredient on the label that I don't have in my pantry." – Registered Dietitian

"Artificial, chemicals, no nutrients, preservatives, refined, fat" – Technology Product Manager

"Anything that is not grown from the earth." – Nursing Home Administrator

"Something that is already mostly prepared...something you just heat up and eat or just eat out of a bag...usually something unhealthy." – Pharmacist

"They grind things up, put fillers/by-products into it to give it bulk, and then reshape it into something they think looks appetizing." – Realtor

"I would describe a 'processed food' as one that has had many of the natural nutrients stripped away, and many unnecessary ingredients added (e.g. dyes, sugar, salt, soy lecithin, etc.)." – Registered Dietitian

"Shitty." – Entrepreneur

"A food that has been altered in
some way – could have been
simply canned, frozen, or man-
made...changed in some way from
the whole, raw food." – Registered
Dietitian

Now compare these definitions to the regulatory
guidelines for processed foods as outlined in The
Federal Food, Drug and Cosmetic Act (SEC. 201. [21
U.S.C. 321]):

"any food other than a raw
agricultural commodity and
includes any raw agricultural
commodity that has been subject
to processing, such as canning,
cooking, freezing, dehydration, or
milling."

According to this definition, cutting corn off the
cob and freezing it makes it processed. Similarly, home-
canning tomato juice on your stove-top using fresh
tomatoes from your garden is also considered
processed. See the dilemma?

Not all processing methods drastically alter foods
or their nutrient composition, nor do all processed foods
include preservatives or other synthetic components.
For example, drying or dehydrating food merely
removes water.

Processing in and of itself isn't the problem. It's when we adopt a predominantly processed eating style that we begin to see negative health consequences. In addition to introducing non-nutritive substances into our bodies, unhealthy processed foods can also displace other nutritious foods in our diet.

Eating "real" seems reasonable in theory, but it isn't always easy. Author Megan Kimble (2015) explored the idea of eating only unprocessed foods for an entire year in her book, *Unprocessed*. Her first challenge was a significant one: to determine the point where a food becomes too processed.

Once her project was completed, she eventually decided to include a few processed foods that she had previously omitted. Her journey highlights the reality that each of us must choose an eating style of our own based on our own beliefs and preferences.

The challenge with eating real food becomes even more significant when we compare modern food preservation practices to the ones of earlier generations. Large-scale manufacturing operations as far back as the Chicago meat-packing days have had quite a different agenda than our grandmothers. Corporate objectives extend beyond preserving nutrients and toward increasing profit margins. The inherent problem with this kind of scaling is that foods must first be broken down into their basic components and then altered in a way that extends their shelf life. Components that spoil quickly are removed, and other ingredients such as fillers, colorings, preservatives and synthetic nutrients are added to create new (and supposedly improved) "products." These food doppelgangers are ubiquitous on grocery shelves today, and clever marketing disguises them well. But looks can be deceiving.

Where has all the real food gone? Farmers' markets are still excellent sources of real food, but you have to look more carefully at the supermarket. Produce, meat, dairy and baked goods are found on the perimeter, while dry beans and other staples can usually be found in the aisles. Even so, the majority of foods that are available are still more processed than they were just a few generations ago.

While much of these changes have been the result of improved technology, we, as consumers, have also driven the change. We steer the industry through our purchases, and essentially we create the demand. We use more convenience products because we've been convinced they save us time, and because we hear our friends talking about them. But the line between real and fake food has become so blurred that we're finding it more and more difficult to remember what unadulterated food looks like. Innately, we all know what real food is, but its packaging sometimes makes it difficult to discern.

Over the years I've worked with patients managing conditions like diabetes, hypertension, renal failure, cancer and other chronic diseases, and I've rarely met an individual who didn't know what healthy food looks like. I would sometimes even ask them directly, "What do you consider healthy?" And almost always, the response would include fruits, vegetables, whole grains, low-fat dairy and lean meats. Very few sugary or heavily processed foods were ever mentioned.

We seem to know what real food is (at least when it's not processed and packaged), we just aren't *choosing* to eat it.

Recently, I saw a commercial claiming "the body's best source of protein is [insert name of well-known dietary supplement retail chain]." Really? The "best" source of protein is a manufactured supplement that comes in a bottle in the form of a powder? Claims like this one make me cringe because they suggest that synthetic products are somehow superior to real food.

The reality is that nutrition is still a young science: the first vitamin was discovered in 1912—just a little over 100 years ago. We're still learning about the synergistic properties of food and how they work together to support our health. Even with our limited understanding of nutrition, it's clear that no single supplement (or real food, for that matter) contains all of the nutrients our body requires. That's why it's critical to include a variety of complex, real foods.

Meal planning is an essential tool for healthy eating, and it's not as difficult as you may think. A seven-day menu can be planned in just 10 to 20 minutes, and having a well-prepared grocery list means trips to the grocery store can take less than an hour each week. I've found that this up-front time investment more than makes up for itself when you consider the alternative: picking up last-minute meals every day during the busy work-week. Meal planning saves time!

Likewise, cooking doesn't have to be as time consuming as many make it out to be. During the week, I like to plan meals that take less than 30 minutes, and I save the more involved meals for the weekends when I have more time.

While clever marketing tactics have convinced us it's easier and faster to buy manufactured food than to prepare homemade meals, it simply isn't true. If you think dining out is a time-saver, consider this: by the time you find parking, wait for a table, place your order, eat your meal, pay the tab and drive home, have you really saved that much time? Convenience meals aren't much better either. Most of them still require some level of preparation, even if it's just taking them out of the package and heating them. And you still have to clean up.

When you consider the cost of health care as a consequence of long-term reliance on unhealthy foods, they aren't cheaper by a long shot. Yes, cooking does require some planning, but the reward is this: higher nutrient quality, increased opportunity for family interaction, and, in some cases, even the generation of less waste.

Real food is a nourishing and delicate part of our ecosystem, but it also provides us with a source of pleasure. In *The Physiology of Taste*, Jean Anthelme Brillat-Savarin (1971) outlined 20 aphorisms around what he referred to as "the pleasures of the table." He also defined what he believed to be the two main functions of taste: It entices us to seek out nourishment and it helps us choose the foods that are best suited to nourish us. As early as 1949, when he first published these observations, he understood that eating involved elements of both art and science.

Carlo Petrini is another proponent of this idea that eating should be pleasurable and that food should be savored. As the well-known organizer of the Slow Food Movement, Petrini (2003) opposes the fast life, using Americans as an example of what happens to the health of a nation when it engages in mindless eating. He also cautions against our tendency toward standardization of food because it promotes flavor "uniformity." In that way, it's easy to understand how many Americans now view food as fuel and nothing more. Pleasure has become secondary, if it's important at all. Take one look at the shelves of any local supermarket and you'll see his point.

One of our biggest challenges with healthy eating is that we have too many choices. Highlighting this reality, Petrini noted that most Americans can have any food in the world delivered to their doorstep within 24-hours. It's all too easy to feed our cravings, regardless of whether they stem from actual physical hunger or not.

A diet is nothing more than a personal eating style—the selection of specific foods based on our beliefs, values, health needs and past exposures to food. Never before has there been a time when we've had more eating styles to choose from: organic, raw, Mediterranean, fat-free, gluten-free, low-carb, low-cholesterol, low-fat, low-protein, low-sodium, low-potassium, low-phosphorus, omnivore, carnivore, vegan, flexitarian, pesco-vegetarian, lacto-vegetarian, pollo-vegetarian, ovo-vegetarian, tyramine-restricted, paleo and the list goes on.

Fortunately, with a little bit of planning we can adequately meet our nutritional needs within the constraints of almost any diet. The challenge arises when we begin combining several restrictions to the degree that we reduce the overall variety of nutrients we allow into our bodies. This is the environment that invites disease.

"Orthorexia" is defined as the preoccupation with healthy eating. Those with orthorexic behaviors often have a long list of foods they "can't" eat. They read labels meticulously to identify potential "bad" foods or ingredients, and they often judge or criticize the food choices of others. While orthorexia isn't yet recognized as a clinical eating disorder, it is felt by some therapists in the field to be an area of increasing concern. In 1997, Steven Bratman introduced the concept of orthorexia to describe individuals who are obsessed with eating to perfection. The word ortho means "right" or "correct" and the following behaviors are examples of possible signs:

- Increasing reliance on supplements to achieve optimal nutrition
- Avoiding a large number of foods without input from a health professional
- Feeling guilty or anxious when deviating from safe foods
- Judging others for not adhering to a similar eating style
- Avoiding foods prepared by others and going out to eat

This idea of eating to perfection is not only impossible, but it can also lead to malnutrition and emotional health issues. Eliminating a large number of foods limits dietary nutrient density, and banning so-called "bad" foods can lead to excluding even some of the healthiest foods over time. This kind of careful selection also requires a great deal of time and energy—which can add stress. If you identified with any of the examples above, you may want to consider talking with your doctor or mental health professional about how to develop a healthy relationship with food.

Eating real food is a simple, inexpensive source of nourishment.

AVOIDING NUTRITIONAL REDUCTIONISM

Today, we use supplements the way some people use fertilizers—carelessly and without fully considering the collateral effects. Instead of replenishing our body's nutrients with real food, we use synthetic chemicals to fill the gaps we create by not eating well. For some, supplements have become an antidote for bad choices—and in extreme cases, an addiction.

While reductionist viewpoints attempt to construct linear (cause and effect) relationships from the smaller components of larger, more complex systems, some researchers believe in the case of nutritional research, the whole is greater than the sum of its parts (Hoffman, 2003). I agree.

We've seen repeatedly that whole systems simply do not behave in a way that can be predicted by piecing together individual parts. Take the glycemic index, for example. Indices have been established for single foods, but when foods are consumed as part of a mixed meal, which is a more realistic pattern of eating, the glycemic index changes dramatically and isn't really all that useful. In the late 90's, as part of my undergraduate coursework, I was a participant in a study that measured the glycemic impact of a new medical food that was designed to reduce night-time hypoglycemia. While the amount of glucose consumed by both sample groups was the same, the mixed meal produced a significantly lower glycemic response. Examining systems as individual parts may be beneficial in some cases, but it can cause us to draw near-sighted, simplistic conclusions that don't necessarily produce benefits in real life.

Several years ago, a well-educated business professional asked me why we couldn't "just put vitamins in candy bars." He wasn't joking. In his mind, since everyone eats candy, it would be a logical solution. He claimed that his busy work schedule didn't allow him the time to eat well, and as a result most of his meals came from a nearby vending machine. I was speechless and it reminded me that sometimes the easiest solution isn't always the best solution. We can do better.

Initially, the purpose of supplements was to enhance the quality of our diets when adequate nutrients were not available, or when medical conditions interfered with nutrient absorption. For that matter, most supplements were designed to correct single nutrient imbalances. They were never intended to nourish us the way real food does. Nevertheless, many products that were once used only for hospitalized patients with serious medical conditions are now available and marketed as a more convenient alternative to meals.

We've learned to dissect foods into their individual parts and then reconstruct them into substances that resemble food. Then we add labels like "functional" foods and add health claims like "strengthens the immune system" to justify the practice. While there is no legal definition of "functional foods" in the U.S., the Academy of Nutrition and Dietetics (formerly the American Dietetic Association) defines them as:

> "whole foods along with fortified, enriched, or enhanced foods that have a potentially beneficial effect on health when consumed as part of a varied diet on a regular basis at effective levels" (Position of the Academy of Nutrition and Dietetics, 2013).

Contrastingly, Marion Nestle (2002) has defined functional foods as products created to be marketed with health claims—there's no doubt these products have become quite profitable for food manufacturers.

In its position paper on nutrient supplementation, The Academy of Nutrition and Dietetics also pointed out that "wise selection of nutrient-rich foods is generally the best strategy for meeting nutrient needs. Foods, particularly plant foods such as fruits, vegetables, whole grains, beans, nuts, seeds, and teas, provide an array of other health-promoting substances beyond vitamins and minerals, including carotenoids and polyphenols such as flavonoids" (Position of the American Dietetic Association, 2009)

These health-promoting substances found in foods are often referred to as "functional foods," though they aren't necessarily restricted to naturally occurring substances. Many functional foods are "modified," meaning they contain enriched ingredients (when nutrients lost during the manufacturing process are added back) or fortified ingredients (when nutrients that were never there to begin with are added—like plant sterols being added to margarines or calcium being added to orange juice). Furthermore, some substances are completely synthetic, such as medical foods designed to treat specific health conditions.

It's important to note that researchers have suggested the health benefits we see with so-called functional foods is more closely related to eating *patterns* rather than any individual nutrient (Lichtenstein & Russel, 2005). Likewise, it's also thought that all foods are functional because of their flavor characteristics, aromatic properties and nutritional composition (Hasler, 2002).

Another unavoidable truth is that we've seen some real failures when it comes to manufactured food. Margarine, high-fructose corn syrup, artificial sweeteners and other well-intentioned fortified foods may have solved a few immediate industry challenges, but they certainly haven't provided much health benefit. And in some cases, we've later learned they have negative health consequences. (Think hydrogenated oils and margarine.)

In reality, everything that has a physical presence is a chemical (Adkins, 1987). One researcher who studies phytochemicals point out that whole foods contain roughly 8,000 of these complex "plant chemicals," and that supplements simply cannot mimic the unique combinations that exist in nature (Liu, 2003). Much of the science around botanicals, and the synergies that exist between the various components, still remains beyond our comprehension. That's precisely why we cannot afford to rely on synthetic forms of nourishment.

In his lengthy 1861 address to a new class of medical students at Harvard, Oliver Wendell Holmes pointed out that "chemistry has grown wise enough to confess the fact of absolute ignorance." He went on to say that "whatever elements nature does not introduce into vegetables, the natural food of all animal life— directly of herbivores, indirectly of carnivorous animals—are to be regarded with suspicion." In 2016, I'm still suspicious.

In *Nourishing Traditions*, author Sally Fallon (1999) recognizes this too. She wrote that "the bewildering array of factors in foods now known to be essential has led well-informed nutritionists to recognize the futility of providing all factors necessary to life in pill form." As a dietitian, I couldn't agree more. It's clear that the best source of nutrition is still found in real, whole foods.

Adding to this confusion, is the very large and powerful (and mostly unregulated) supplement industry. The idea that supplements are necessary for everyone, regardless of health status, is a slippery slope. I once met with a salesperson who tried his best to convince me that mangosteen juice cured cancer. Not only did he lack scientific evidence for his statements, relying on testimonials instead, he defended this fact by explaining that the company had a patented proprietary process for extracting the pericarp—the source of the elusive active ingredient. Conveniently, the details of this process remained unclear, yet he couldn't understand why I would question its status as a "superfood" with extraordinary health benefits. And he certainly had no idea how to answer my question about why mangosteen juice was better than, say, orange juice or any other fruit for that matter. When we glorify single foods, or single components of foods, we miss the point.

The Academy of Nutrition and Dietetics states that "the best nutrition-based strategy for promoting optimal health and reducing the risk of chronic disease is to wisely choose a wide variety of nutrient-rich foods" (Position of the American Dietetic Association: Nutrient Supplementation, 2009). Likewise, the Dietary Guidelines for Americans (DGA) has offered similar advice in the past, but the most recent release was noticeably different. In 2005, this was the message:

> "A basic premise of the Dietary Guidelines is that nutrient needs should be met primarily through

consuming foods. Foods provide an array of nutrients and other compounds that may have beneficial effects on health. In certain cases, fortified foods and dietary supplements may be useful sources of one or more nutrients that otherwise might be consumed in less than recommended amounts. *However, dietary supplements, while recommended in some cases, cannot replace a healthful diet.*"

In 2015, the DGA still encouraged choosing healthy foods and beverages rather than supplements, but there was a clear shift in the overall context of the message:

"Nutritional needs should be met primarily from foods. Individuals should aim to meet their nutrient needs through healthy eating patterns that include nutrient-dense foods. Foods in nutrient-dense forms contain essential vitamins and minerals and also dietary fiber and other naturally occurring substances that may have positive health effects. In some cases, fortified foods and

dietary supplements may be useful
in providing one or more nutrients
that otherwise may be consumed
in less than recommended
amounts."

The excerpt "supplements cannot replace a healthful diet" is mysteriously missing in the latest release. But why? I might understand if there had been significant research developments in the last decade to support the beneficial role of supplements within the generally healthy population—but that isn't the case. This leads me to believe there were other driving factors behind the revision. It's no secret that the supplement industry is highly profitable—and that means it's also highly influential.

While this may be true, supplements aren't universally bad. In fact, some nutritional supplements are medically necessary. When used properly—to fill known and verified nutrient gaps—they can be an integral part of a comprehensive self-care practice. Just eight months after moving to Seattle from Austin, my vitamin D level plummeted from 34 to 20. While there are differing opinions as to what constitutes a "normal" level, mine was certainly on the low end of normal—and it had declined significantly from *my* normal level in the past. Considering the geographical change that precipitated the decline, it's not all that surprising. Not only are there less sunny days in Seattle compared to Austin, but the sunshine just isn't as intense due to the latitude.

At any rate, my medical provider suggested, and I agreed, that additional Vitamin D was warranted, and I decided to add a supplement to my daily routine in the winter months when sunshine is minimal. Supplements are intended to fill specific nutrient gaps, not to be used as a crutch for unhealthy eating styles or to cure medical illnesses that aren't directly related to nutrient deficiencies.

Complementary medicine is the norm in many parts of the world, and while some practices are not equally regarded by all medical professionals, many of them have endured for generations within various cultures across the globe. In *Green Pharmacy*, Barbara Griggs (1997) paints a vivid picture of the history of medicine. In the early days, and also in indigenous societies, herbs were the primary healing agents. And still today, most of our medications are synthesized from plants.

Plants have baffled researchers for years. Like animals, plants are comprised of many complex chemical compounds—not single active ingredients like supplements. We know that the combination of compounds act differently when consumed together, as with a whole plant or a whole meal. But when they are separated into individual parts, the outcome is altered.

The Dalai Lama also sees the fallacy in our reliance on synthetic foods. In *The Art of Happiness*, he points out that Western thinking assumes that "everything can be accounted for" (Lama & Cutler, 1998). We simply don't know what we don't know, and the world is a much more complex place than we will probably ever fully understand. That's reason enough to see the value of real, whole food over the adulterated alternatives we see on retail shelves today.

When I started my career over 15 years ago, I was the prototypical clinical dietitian. I followed all the rules. Diet recommendations were dictated by protocols, precise mathematical calculations and solid scientific research. As a consultant for several long-term care facilities, my job was to ensure that residents were being offered diets that not only helped them maintain good health, but ideally helped them improve it. But chronic medical conditions frequently made this challenging, especially since many of the treatments included dietary restrictions.

I remember one resident vividly. She was undergoing dialysis treatment and wasn't eating well. After carefully studying her lab values, I constructed what I thought to be the perfect diet. It consisted of a laundry list of foods that she should not eat. If it was high in potassium, forget it. High in phosphorus? No way. I can't even remember how many restrictions I listed, but it was extensive. I confidently faxed over my recommendations to the physician, satisfied that I had just executed the most evidence-based recommendation possible. It was perfect! Of course it would be approved. I had thought of everything!

I was crushed when the fax was returned with the words, "What's, left sawdust?" scrawled across the top. (Clearly not approved.)

That physician knew something that I hadn't quite figured out yet, and I realized at that moment (thankfully early on in my career) that good medical care is not about know-it-all providers dictating what patients *should* do to care for themselves. Good medical care considers what makes life enjoyable, and in extreme cases of illness, what makes it bearable. What's right isn't always perfect, and what's perfect isn't always right. Every time I see sawdust I'm reminded of this lesson.

Throughout history, eating has been as much about celebrating life's beautiful moments as it has been about nourishment. The sharing of meals brings families and communities together to solve problems, share knowledge and offer support and encouragement.

The reality is that we cannot manufacture and bottle what we haven't yet discovered. Until we have a more solid understanding of the synergistic effects of food, we're short-changing ourselves when we rely on synthetic products. Nevertheless, there are many different viewpoints when it comes to healthy eating, and each of us must decide for ourselves how to best nourish our body.

MOVING

Most people understand that in addition to eating well, physical activity is also essential for optimal health. Movement fuels brain function, helps move oxygen to our cells and aids in the regeneration and repair of cells. Our level of fitness also affects our ability to carry out our unique purpose, and it can either be an agent for positive change or a limiting factor.

Systemic Health

The Centers for Disease Control (CDC) recommends that adults accumulate at least 150 minutes of moderate-intensity aerobic physical activity each week, along with two or more days of muscle-strengthening activities that include all major muscle groups. That may sound like a lot, but broken down it's really just 30 minutes, five days each week. As with our food choices, how we move our body is also dependent on our personal style and preferences.

I despise running. I mean, I really hate it. Even so, I somehow managed to complete a 5K one summer simply because I wanted to cross it off my bucket list. But I didn't enjoy a single minute of it. Exercising as part of a group has always been much more enjoyable for me. There's just something encouraging and motivating about being in a room full of other high-energy individuals that makes it more fun. When we find something we love, our likelihood of sustaining new habits is much greater. Fortunately, it's not necessary for all of us to be ultra-marathoners or intense body builders to realize the health benefits of physical activity. Experimenting with different types of activities can be a great way to get started, or to add variety to long-standing routines.

Sedentary lifestyles are becoming more common as technology enables more people to accomplish work tasks without leaving their chair. And as our commutes become longer, the time we spend sitting behind the wheel also increases periods of inactivity.

"Sitting is the new smoking," a phrase coined by Dr. James Levine, began circulating back in 2014 to point out the dangers associated with sedentary lifestyles

(Park, 2014). Several years earlier, the 2003-2004 National Health and Nutrition Examination Survey revealed that both children and adults spent nearly 55% of their waking hours engaged in sedentary behaviors (Matthews, Chen, Freedson, et al., 2008). Our increasingly inactive lifestyles are taking a toll. A study in 2009 showed that extended periods of sitting were associated with elevated risks of mortality from cardiovascular disease (Katzmarzyk, Church, Craig & Bouchard, 2009).

Getting started (or restarted in many cases) with physical activity is often the hardest part. With this in mind, it's smart to avoid missing two consecutive days of doing some kind of activity—even if it's just taking a short walk.

When working with clients who have weight loss goals, I've found that focusing first on physical activity often leads to better results. The reason? Being active reduces our response to visual food cues (Evaro, 2012), which might explain why donuts aren't quite as tempting after an intense workout.

The simple lesson here is: "Move more, sit less."

WALKING

The National Weight Control Registry, an ongoing research study that gathers data about people who have successfully lost 30 pounds or more and kept it off for at least a year, found the most frequently reported form of activity was walking.

Walking is natural, and it's one of the simplest forms of physical activity—even for those with the busiest of lifestyles. (Incidentally, I wrote much of this book while walking on my treadmill!)

With the exception of athletic shoes, walking doesn't require any special equipment or membership fees. This makes it especially popular among individuals who are trying to leave their sedentary routines behind in pursuit of better health. Walking can be done almost anywhere and it doesn't require much preparation.

For those who are intense exercisers, walking may not seem like it could provide significant health benefits, but it really just depends on what you're trying to accomplish. While it certainly won't prepare you for the rigors of an Iron Man competition, it can help reduce stress, improve cardiovascular health and offer opportunities to spend time with family and friends. For someone who is just getting started with physical activity, walking is a great choice.

YOGA

One of the first things I did on my sabbatical was enroll in a six-week beginner's yoga class. It helped me learn more about my body, as well as how to use my breath to reduce tension and experience a sense of calm.

Most of us tend to avoid things that are challenging—especially when those things interfere with our free time—but there's something really special about the feeling you get when you nail a pose, or realize you did it better than you did the last time. Rising to challenges helps us build confidence, and yoga has a way of prompting us to engage in other healthy activities as well.

Yoga has helped me understand more clearly that I am, and will always be, a work in progress. It has also helped me understand that I'm not alone; everyone else is a work in progress too. This special form of physical activity interconnects many, if not all, of the eight self-care dimensions. Yoga is a practice that brings the concept of self-care together.

RESTING

We all need to retreat from life's demands periodically. Time away allows us to reconnect with our personal values and assess the current direction of our lives. We need this time to evaluate whether we are moving toward the things we want in our life or whether we are moving away from them. Checking in regularly helps us avoid wasting our valuable time and energy on things that don't matter much in the long term.

But rest isn't necessarily idleness. Sometimes rest is taking a break from some of our habits and redirecting our energy toward forming new ones. In that regard, rest has the potential to make us more productive.

As early as the 1960's, when the wellness movement was just beginning, Norman Vincent Peale recognized the value of taking breaks to "occasionally retreat from the world, in order to live effectively in the world" (Peale, 1967). This observation was made even before the arrival of incessant technological distractions, which have become significant sources of tension and anxiety today. As a culture, we burn daylight at both ends. Even the twilight hours are now illuminated by the glow of electronic devices, stealing precious hours of our sleep.

Slowing down is a scary thing for those who are used to being busy, but resting is an important component of our systemic health. There are several ways we can incorporate more rest into our lives:

MASSAGE

We often associate massage with luxurious (and expensive) spa treatments, but it can be a surprisingly affordable way to reduce stress and relieve muscle tension. As part of my own self-care practice, I schedule a massage every month and I categorize it under "health care" within my home budget. To me, it's that important.

My first massage was a gift from my husband on my 30th birthday. I can still remember the feeling of extreme relaxation (something my type "A" nature has made nearly impossible for me to experience). And at roughly a dollar a minute, which is typical of many membership-based companies, it's still much cheaper than its alternative: medical care. Ongoing chronic muscle tension and stress can lead to pain and stiffness, which limit mobility. And when you consider the cost associated with meeting insurance deductibles, co-insurance, copays and treatments like physical therapy, it's well worth the cost. Massage is an enjoyable investment too.

Sleep

The importance of rest has received more attention in recent years. Sufficient sleep is essential for us to recover from both the mental and physical demands of living. When we're well-rested, we're better able to solve problems, make decisions and handle competing priorities. The National Institutes of Health recommend that adults get at least seven to eight hours of sleep each day (National Heart, Lung, Blood Institute, 2016).

Studies have shown that lack of adequate sleep is linked to obesity (due to changes in eating habits which often results in higher calorie consumption), and with obesity rates climbing, medical conditions such as sleep apnea have also caused sleep disturbances.

Sleep is indeed a vital component of good health.

Time Off

Taking time off is yet another way we can create an environment for rest. Once-relished vacations are no longer an escape from the daily grind as mobile devices enable us to work anywhere, anytime (and all the time). Sadly, that's the expectation in many work environments. Many people never go on vacation, much less take a temporary break from employment. Instead, they take their work with them and remain "on call," feeling guilty if they don't respond to messages immediately. Honestly, I think employers should feel embarrassed for encouraging—and in some cases even rewarding—this kind of behavior. Retreating from the

Treatments for chronic medical conditions range from taking medication to undergoing invasive procedures, and it's important to have a clear understanding of how each option might impact our life differently. This is also why establishing a relationship of trust with your medical care team a critical aspect of a comprehensive self-care plan.

BALANCING

The concept of work/life balance has been met with some controversy. Critics believe there is no such thing because balance implies an equal distribution of time and energy (an ideal that is simply unrealistic). While it may not be attainable in its purest sense, balance is a term that we often apply to the decisions we make about how to divide our time. Giving adequate attention to the things that are important to us—our family, our life partner, our friends and career—may not require our equal attention to feel balanced.

Ultimately, balance is a perception. Each of us spends our time where we feel it needs to be spent. Setting boundaries around our relationships and responsibilities helps us discern when enough is enough, as well as when we may need to push a little harder.

Despite the fact that technology has made us more productive, it seems our demands continue to grow, especially in the workplace. As a corporate wellness health coach, I've heard from numerous employees that they eat lunch at their desks (or don't eat at all) because they're afraid they might get overlooked for a promotion. They fear their absence may suggest they are less engaged and dedicated than their peers.

More and more forward-thinking employers are taking a new stance on paid time off. Unlimited vacation policies and "get your work done and take off when you want to" philosophies send a positive message to employees that they are trusted, and that high performers are rewarded for hard work. All of us need to recharge our batteries periodically to perform at our best, and smart employers are noticing this trend. Likewise, smart employees are joining companies with this kind of philosophy.

Ultimately, our habits around eating, moving and resting determine our physical abilities to reach our goals and live our purpose.

or remove—we sometimes forget what we do want in our life.

With this newfound interest in positive psychology, I eventually decided to close my private practice as a nutrition therapist and explore the science of motivational interviewing and behavior change. As a new health coach, this experience helped me build a more unique skillset by blending traditional preventive health care approaches with behavior change theory. This also enabled me to help people more effectively turn their intentions into actions that made sense to them personally.

I noticed immediately that these new techniques were much more practical and effective than the widely accepted health education model I had been using over the last decade. One reason coaching is more effective is that it's more conversational than traditional counseling methods, which can often feel prescriptive and judgmental. One of the hallmarks of coaching is that the responsibility for setting the agenda and focus of change lies with the individual, not the coach. People are much more likely to take action when they choose the focus and boundaries for the goals they select. For example, I may think it's in your best interest to reduce saturated fat to reduce your cholesterol level, but you may find the idea of increasing physical activity more appealing. For years, health care professionals have imposed treatments and behaviors on their patients without getting adequate buy-in. (I know because I was one of them.) It's no surprise, then, that sustained behavior change continues to be a challenge for many patients and providers. An authoritative approach usually just creates resistance. No one likes being told what do to, no matter how old they are or how ill they may be.

I'm confident that in the coming years we will see a shift away from the traditional "provider" approach, and toward a more holistic, "partnership" style of healthcare. We believe what we hear ourselves say out loud, and if we can imagine ourselves doing something successfully, we're much more likely to take action toward a goal. Our belief in ourselves—in our ability to achieve our goals—is directly related to our level of self-confidence. When our self-confidence is high, we are much more successful, but when our self-confidence is low, we may not even try.

Positive psychology is empowering, and the idea of developing our strengths rather than fixing our flaws is brilliant. With this mindset, even if we don't achieve our goals we're still able to grow from our attempts. We become more open to learning, and more adept at adjusting our goals so that we can try again. Strengths are resources and our attempts to reach our goals are simply experiments. Maintaining a spirit of positivity propels us forward.

So what exactly is positivity? While the term isn't new, it still isn't well-defined. Its origin dates back to 1659 when Henry Hickman wrote about the "positivity of sin." Likewise, within the scientific community, electropositivity is a chemistry term long-used to describe the reactive properties of elements.

More recently, positive psychology researchers found that having a 3:1 ratio of positive to negative emotions is predictive of "flourishing," which has been defined as a state of being that goes beyond happiness

(Fredrickson, 2013). Flourishing includes both *feeling* good and *doing* good.

While other researchers have since called their methods into question, there still appears to be merit in the idea that positive emotions help build resilience (Brown, et al., 2013). Even the researchers who debunked the study's methodology didn't dispute the overall outcome of the study. There seems to be consensus that flourishing occurs when our positive emotions outweigh our negative ones.

In the context of research, positivity is often described as having a high level of positive emotions. From a self-care perspective, positivity can be as a catalyst for purposeful living. It's the spark that ignites possibilities and transforms our intentions into actions. In this way, positivity is positive thinking in action. With a positive mindset, we can see and focus on what is good and more effectively work through life's difficulties.

In many ways, positivity is grounded optimism. For one thing, positive people don't ignore the negative things in life. They accept them, find solutions to their problems and move forward. Instead of dwelling on what isn't good, they learn from their experiences and continue to move forward.

Being "grounded" means being able to see both the bright side and the dark side of every situation. It's okay to wear rose-colored glasses every now and then, but sometimes you have to take them off to see the world as it truly is. Dwelling on the darkness, however, never solves anything.

Maintaining a spirit of positivity in the face of life's often overwhelming disappointments can be difficult, but not impossible. We know this because we've seen resilient individuals overcome some of life's most extraordinary challenges time and time again.

Viktor Frankl survived imprisonment in a Nazi concentration camp; Randy Pausch used his terminal diagnosis as a teaching platform; and most of us probably have friends, colleagues or neighbors who have refused to live as a victim of their circumstances. They may fall down, but they always find a way to get back up. While it's hard to see when we're deep within the eye of the storm, hardships help us grow and become better at living, better at accepting our mistakes and better at celebrating our successes.

"That which does not kill me, makes me stronger," a quote that was popularized by the German philosopher Nietzsche, is a great illustration of this point. Suffering forces us to grow. Abraham Maslow, who is known for establishing the famous hierarchy of needs, also felt that "our suffering and challenges serve to bring out greater strengths." In other words, there always seems to be a purpose behind our suffering.

Within each of us, regardless of our genetic makeup or environmental factors, lies the ability to overcome obstacles. Resiliency, optimism, determination, hope, mental toughness—whatever you choose to call it, with practice we can gradually develop a positive, solution-oriented mindset and avoid falling into the helpless role of victim. In this way, we can learn not to allow life's obstacles to stand in the way of accomplishing our goals, and we can learn to work with and through difficulties rather than complain about them.

If positivity exists on a spectrum, then it's easy to understand how each of us might use it differently. Positivity can be applied in an infinite number of ways across each of the eight dimensions of self-care: how we eat, move and rest; how we express ourselves; how we illuminate our inner truth; how we allocate our resources; how we think; how we contribute to the world; how we connect with others and how we harmonize with nature.

I noticed recently during a visit to Barnes and Noble that they have changed their signage from "self-help" to "personal growth." I think it's a much better descriptor, because it changes a somewhat negative label to one that is more positive. Personally, I have felt the weight of imperfection while perusing the shelves for "self-help" books in the past. It was an unpleasant reminder of the fact that there were areas of my life that needed to be "fixed."

Positivity unlocks possibilities. It makes crazy ideas seem not so crazy anymore. It makes audacious goals seem attainable. It makes difficult and awkward conversations constructive and life-changing. And it allows us to build lives and communities that are supportive and mutually beneficial.

But is it possible to be too positive? Maybe. Research has shown that greater life satisfaction is correlated to the *frequency* of positive emotions rather than their *intensity* (Diener, Sandvik, et al., 1991). It seems being mostly positive is more beneficial than being intensely positive.

Our level of positivity does have an effect on our health. One study found that women who displayed cynical hostility were more likely to have a higher cancer mortality and poor cardiovascular health (Tindle, Chang, Kuller, et al., 2009). Our mindset—how we see and interpret the world—seems to make a difference when it comes to health.

Positivity is also contagious, something I happen to find particularly encouraging. Research has shown that people who are low in positivity perform better when other people in their group are higher in positivity (Livi, Alessandri, Caprarab & Pierro, 2015). This can be quite beneficial when large, diverse groups are working toward a common goal. Perhaps one bad apple doesn't always spoil the bunch.

Positivity may seem to come naturally to some people, but most of us have to work at it.

BEING OPTIMISTIC

Optimism is a field of psychological research that studies positive expectations about the future. It has been suggested that optimistic people exert more effort, whereas their counterparts (pessimists) tend to disengage from it (Carver & Scheier, 2014). Optimists are said to have positive outlooks about their future (Carver, Scheier & Segerstrom, 2010). A hallmark characteristic of an optimist is the ability to depict vivid mental images of positive events in the future (Blackwell, Rius-Ottenheim, Maaren, et al., 2012), and the more vivid the image, the more optimistic the individual is said to be.

But there's a catch. Optimistic thinking without the behavior to back it up isn't all that useful. Our actions and interactions must match our optimistic mindset to provide any real health benefits. Our ability to persevere in the face of difficulty is what makes optimism such an asset. One study found that it may even be possible to prevent depression through building optimism (Seligman, Schulman, DeRubeis & Hollon, 1999).

Setting realistic expectations, and being willing to make adjustments when necessary, is another characteristic of an optimist.

The following activities can be used to develop and enhance optimism and positivity:

JOURNALING

Journaling is a powerful outlet for our emotions, especially for those who tend to be more private and less likely to share their feelings openly. Translating our feelings into words can be therapeutic. Many times, I have felt my frustrations dissipate as I write them on paper. Writing also allows us to vent negative thoughts without becoming fixated on them or allowing them to intensify by talking about them. In that way, journaling helps us put our thoughts to rest without giving them a voice. Likewise, the process of putting our thoughts on paper also helps us bring ideas to life by enabling us to clarify our intentions and set meaningful goals.

WRITING LETTERS OF GRATITUDE

Crafting hand-written letters is somewhat of a lost art. It takes effort to pen our thoughts on paper, particularly when we are used to reading and writing concise, direct emails. (There's no delete button either.) Written gratitude is a positive expression of emotion that brings as much joy to the giver as it does to the receiver. If you're grateful for something, say so.

COUNTING BLESSINGS

Making a list of the good things in life can be an effective way to enhance positivity. It helps us stay focused on what's going well rather than what isn't.

Interestingly, though, it seems there may be an upper limit. One study found that counting our blessings more than three times each week appears to be less effective at enhancing optimism than doing it just once each week (Lyubomirsky, Sheldon & Schkade, 2005). This calls into question whether there is a threshold when it comes to reflecting on the good.

It has also been suggested that this exercise helps us see that many of our blessings come as a result of our own efforts (Miller, 2009), which can help us develop higher levels of self-confidence and motivation to pursue goals as well.

PERFORMING ACTS OF KINDNESS

Random acts of kindness, such as opening the door for someone or buying coffee for a stranger, can be gratifying—for both for the giver and receiver of the kindness. Think about the last time you were the recipient of an unexpected kindness. How did you feel? And when was the last time you performed a kindness without expecting anything in return? How did you feel then?

IMAGINING YOUR IDEAL FUTURE SELF

As discussed earlier, our mental images are powerful. When we paint vivid pictures in our mind about who we want to be in the future, we can begin focusing our attention on finding creative ways to invite those images into our reality. Envisioning our future is a powerful motivator for change. This exercise can be easily incorporated into a meditation practice or other daily routine.

DEALING WITH NEGATIVITY

As I was working on this chapter at a local coffee shop, there was a group of ladies sitting at the table next to me who appeared to be having a discussion about a book they had just read. The conversation started out with several complaints about their daughters-in-law, specifically around their parenting methods, but eventually moved on to topics like living with intention and creating more meaningful connections with friends and family. I realized that sometimes we really do just need to vent so that we can move on to other, more meaningful things. Having a supportive group of friends gives us that platform.

While supportive environments can help us process negativity, it seems that some people still prefer to focus on the downside of life: the reasons something won't work, the hopelessness of a problem, or any statement followed by the word "but." It's almost as if they are drawn to the negative side of situations. These personalities, often referred to as Debbie Downers and Negative Nancys, can erode personal relationships and cause them to be alienated by some groups.

Still, it begs the question, "Are there benefits to being negative?" Some research has shown that we may be genetically predisposed to seeking out negative aspects because it helps us identify potential dangers—a classic survival mechanism. Even so, the tendency to be negative appears to do more harm than good when it comes to discovering and living our purpose.

Will Bowen (2007), author of *A Complaint Free World*, quickly realized that his habit of complaining became more prevalent when he was around other complainers. His strategy for breaking the habit of complaining works something like this: every time we verbalize a complaint, we simply switch a bracelet from one wrist to the other. This exercise helps us become more aware of our own negative behaviors—and also the specific situations in which these behaviors are more likely occur. Bowen noticed that his typical pattern of conversation with certain people seemed to frequently revolve around complaining; and while he felt guilty at first, he ultimately decided he needed to limit his interactions with them in order to improve his own sense of positivity. According to Bowen, complaining is talking about things you do not want rather than the things you do. If the ultimate goal is to cultivate more of what you want, then focusing on what you don't want is counterproductive.

I made the decision to take a break from social media after realizing it had become a significant source of negativity for me. It was one of my first exercises in self-care. Complaining, a form of negativity, is highly contagious, weaving itself into our personal and professional relationships, and preventing us from creating meaningful connections. As Bowen noted, merely "thinking" about complaining is much less toxic than actually releasing it into the world. We all have transitory negative thoughts, but how we choose to respond to them impacts our emotive health.

This is not to say that we should ostracize people simply because they don't believe what we believe. People who have differing views on life—even ones we may perceive as being negative—can provide meaningful perspectives that help us grow personally. I have friends who are optimistic and friends who are pessimistic, though it's probably no surprise that I find it much easier to interact with the optimists. That said, I still appreciate friends who aren't afraid to express their feelings—even when they happen to do so in a negative way. I understand that sometimes we all need to vent, and sometimes we just need someone to listen as we work through life's difficult situations. That is how we support one another. But when I notice that the negativity of others has a negative impact on my life, I begin to set boundaries.

FINDING MEANING

In *Man's Search for Meaning*, author Viktor E. Frankl (2006) describes his experience living in a German concentration camp. He used optimism, hope, art, humor, connectedness, creativity, detachment, solitude and grit as survival skills. Frankl wrote "...everything can be taken from a man but one thing: the last of the human freedoms—to choose one's attitude in any given set of circumstances..." His heart-wrenching, yet empowering experience served as a lesson to all of us that developing a positive mindset in the face of immense suffering is possible. His story shows that our chosen mindset is directly related to our level of happiness—and essentially to our very survival. We all experience suffering. In fact, Frankl believed that all suffering is equal because every person that suffers experiences real pain, no matter what the level of pain. Frankl's experience is one of the most powerful human stories I've ever read. Suffering is a human condition, but it's what we do with our suffering that makes the difference. His story reminds us that each of us has a specific mission to carry out in life. In that regard, it also means that, as individuals, we are irreplaceable. Our unique contribution cannot be created by anyone else, nor can it be repeated. Your purpose may be discovered by answering this simple question: What would the world lose or miss out on if you never existed?

According to Frankl's Logotherapy (meaning-centered psychology), there are three ways we can discover meaning: 1) by creating something; 2) by experiencing something; or 3) by our attitude when we suffer (Frankl, 2006). What will your story be? What do you want the culmination of your life to reveal or leave behind as a legacy?

If you haven't yet seen *The Last Lecture* by Randy Pausch (2007), then I encourage you to watch it. It is one of the most moving testimonies I've ever seen. None of us will live forever; that is the one certainty we have as human beings. But experiencing a meaningful life isn't about living forever, it's about living a life of greatness while we are able. With the knowledge that his remaining days were limited after being diagnosed with terminal cancer, Pausch chose to use that experience in a positive way. In his last lecture, he encouraged all of us to pursue our childhood dreams and support the dreams of others. What are your dreams?

IN PRACTICE

What, Why, How, Do It Now!

What specifically about your emotive health needs the most attention? For example: expressing your feelings more effectively, addressing a tendency to complain, expressing gratitude, communicating effectively with others, finding meaning and purpose, etc.

Why is this specific area of your emotive health so important to you right now? Are there significant consequences at stake if you do not address your concerns? Would an improvement in your health allow you to accomplish something that you haven't been able to up until now?

How could you improve your emotive health? Try to come up with at least three ideas.

Do It Now! Take one step right now, even if it's small: schedule an appointment with a professional counselor, create a calendar reminder for meditation, write a reminder on a post-it note, call a friend to ask for their support, etc.

CHAPTER 3: LUMINESCENT HEALTH

LUMINESSENCE: HOW WE ILLUMINATE OUR INNER TRUTH

The luminescent dimension of self-care pertains to our "inner light" or "inner truth." It's the internal compass that guides us from within, helping us interpret the world through our own unique lens. Our inner truth is what we believe in passionately.

Some refer to this inner light as "spirituality," and, while our inner light certainly can reflect aspects of our spiritual beliefs, our luminessence is more complex than that. Our "self" is our "essence." It's the unchanging nature of our being. It's who we are at our core. I coined the word luminessence to describe the connection between our inner guiding light (lumen) and our unchanging nature (essence).

This dimension helps us make decisions about how we live, and it's not surprising that it often points each of us in different directions since it's constructed using our unique principles, values, skills, personal experiences and interests. Our luminessence is a reflection of our personal truth and we use it as a filter to make sense of the world around us.

Our luminessence is what people see behind our eyes when we smile. It's the light we emit when we live authentically and when we express our "self" without limitation.

The reason this aspect of our health is so important is that it's often neglected. Rather than exposing our truth, we tend to conform to societal expectations. The trouble with this is that our luminessence acts like a buoy. We may be able to submerge it for a while, but eventually it will surface. Truth floats. We desperately need to express our authenticity.

The primary self-care practices that influence our luminescent health are:

Being Authentic
Cultivating Self-Awareness
Changing Our Behaviors
Enjoying the Moment
Playing

BEING AUTHENTIC

Being authentic is living unapologetically true to who we are. It isn't just about telling *the* truth; it's about telling *our* truth. In *The Gifts of Imperfection*, Brené Brown (2010) refers to authenticity as a daily practice of "letting go of who we think we're supposed to be and embracing who we are." When we care more about living our truth than what others think, we're living authentically. Sometimes I think we get so caught up in what others think of us that we ignore our inner truth.

I've noticed throughout my life that I've always been drawn to people who possess positive energy. There's something magnetic about them, and it's hard not to want what they have. They are fearless. Bold. Optimistic. Futuristic. And they exude authenticity!

Whether or not they show it, they aren't oblivious or immune to life's tribulations. They recognize that the world is full of struggles, but instead of wasting their time complaining or dwelling on what they cannot change, they focus on finding solutions to problems they can change. They see problems as opportunities to learn and grow rather than casting blame on others or making excuses. They use positivity as a tool by rolling up their sleeves and getting to work.

Being authentic does not, however, require us to reveal every detail of our lives. Dialing down our story isn't being insincere; it can sometimes just mean we're emotionally intelligent enough to be respectful of others. Not every story needs to be told (or heard for that matter). When being authentic feels more like airing our dirty laundry, venting or complaining, it might not really be authenticity that we're expressing. In some cases, journaling or talking with a professional counselor might make more sense.

When there are inconsistencies between what we say and what we do, others will question our authenticity. A woman once shared with me that after being continuously criticized by her personal trainer for her poor food choices, she bumped into him at the grocery store. Not only was she mortified by the amount of junk food she saw in his cart—some of the very same things he had disparaged her for eating—she was equally shocked by his response to her discovery. "This is what weekends are for," he said. She was disappointed, to say the least, but she also began to doubt his authenticity—and credibility. She had to reconsider whether his recommendations were sound, or even attainable.

Authentic people aren't afraid to admit their mistakes. They aren't ashamed of their imperfections and they don't place unrealistic expectations on others. Imperfections are what make us uniquely human. Acknowledging them takes away their power. In fact, sometimes laughing about our mistakes can even be therapeutic. I once backed into the garage door because I was in such a hurry that I forgot to press the silly button. Was it embarrassing? Sure. Do my husband and I still laugh about it every now and then? Absolutely.

Being able to admit our weaknesses is a sign of strength. When we give our imperfections a gentle hug, accepting they are part of who we are rather than trying to conceal or punish ourselves for their existence, we can move on to more meaningful things.

When we're authentic—no longer trying to suppress aspects of our "self" that we don't feel are socially acceptable—our inner truth naturally bubbles to the surface.

CULTIVATING SELF-AWARENESS

Being authentic requires us to have an intimate connection with ourselves. As silly as that may sound, many of us are too "busy" to spend much time alone. Had I realized earlier that there was such a disconnect between my luminessence and my career, I probably would have resigned sooner.

We become more aware when we give our full attention to our surroundings. On a recent flight, I began reading Jon Kabat-Zinn's (1994) book, *Wherever You Go, There You Are.* In it he urges: "Stop trying to get somewhere. Be where you are already." When the book was written, I was a junior in high school and had never even heard of meditation.

For the first time, I made a real effort to be aware—from an altitude of 37,000 feet. I heard the voice of a flight attendant overhead, the rumbling of the plane's engine, the clicking of doors in the galley and the faint sound of music coming from my husband's headphones. As my ears popped, I noticed The Trey Anastasio Band album cover glowing from the screen on his phone. I felt the crunch of pretzels between my teeth and the sting of Prosecco bubbles on my tongue. And then...turbulence. I bobbed in my seat as if we were driving a truck over a street full of potholes, and then I noticed from my window that it was raining sideways (obviously due to the speed of the plane). It was still strange. And as we descended, I watched the rain change to into a gray and then white, fluffy snow.

Had I not chosen to be mindful, I may have only focused on the words in the book, never realizing that anything else was happening around me. Being self-aware requires stillness.

Sitting with ourselves in quiet with nothing to "do" can be unsettling at first. I know because it was one of the most difficult things I experienced at the beginning of my sabbatical. A thousand thoughts rushed through my brain and all I could think about was, "Why am I just sitting here?" Every one of us is a unique being with unique gifts to share with the world, but unless we understand those gifts intimately, it can be pretty hard to share them. This is why having an awareness of our "self" is so important.

When we become self-aware, we sometimes gloss over our strengths, gifts and talents. We don't see the possibilities that might come from using them differently. Focusing on how to use our strengths and gifts can often produce empowering insights and ideas.

Self-awareness can sometimes highlight our flaws, but not all of our flaws need to be fixed. It's up to each of us to carefully choose which aspects of our "self" we want to cultivate and which ones we will choose to ignore. For example, some people prefer solitude and experience high levels of anxiety in social settings. When this preference is viewed as a "flaw," however, they may try to "fix" it by forcing themselves to attend social events and gatherings even though it makes them miserable. While some level of interaction with other people is certainly healthy, forcing ourselves to be something we aren't or to enjoy something we don't isn't being authentic.

Being self-aware also means being in touch with our intuition. I've learned to listen to the little voice inside me and use it as a guide. Only when I've ignored it have I met disappointment. Self-awareness isn't just about identifying the areas of our lives we want to change—like when we track our steps using a pedometer or use a diary to log our food choices. Sometimes enhanced awareness helps us simply understand ourselves more clearly. This often leads to our acceptance of what *is*. Not everything we become aware of needs to be changed.

We use self-awareness to create a deeper connection with our luminessence, and there are many ways we can do this:

SELF-REFLECTION

Writing down our thoughts helps us become more aware of them without having to consider how they might be received by someone else. Just as with expressing our emotions, keeping a journal helps us reflect on our thoughts as well as assess our progress toward goals. The format doesn't seem to matter. In fact, research has shown similar weight loss outcomes among individuals who use either pen and paper or internet diaries (Yu, Sealey-Potts & Rodriguez, 2015).

Creating milestones and measuring our progress along the way keeps us moving toward our goals.

Self-Assessment

Self-assessments are tools that help us better understand who we are. While no assessment can define us completely, they do provide us with insights about why we *think*, *say*, and *do* the things we do. Self-assessments can be particularly helpful when we find ourselves "stuck," either personally or professionally. Likewise, assessments can help us examine our life satisfaction, happiness or even personality traits. This is especially helpful as we consider how to best communicate with others.

Meditation

Meditation is a widely practiced wellness tool that can help us establish a deeper connection with our authentic "self." Furthermore, evidence supports a link between meditation, a strong immune system and cardiovascular health (Kok, Waugh & Fredrickson, 2013). It enables us to reflect on what's most important to us, to ask questions about whether our life aligns with our inner truth and what (if any) changes might need to be made to bring us closer to that truth. If you are new to meditation, taking a class, using an app or listening to a guided recording can help build a personal practice. Stillness is an art, though it does take time and repetition to master. We'll explore meditation more in chapter 5.

CHANGING OUR BEHAVIORS

When we recognize a disconnect between what we *want* and what *is*, we have a three clear choices.

One, we can do nothing. Instead of taking action, we can accept what *is* and embrace our reality. This option is especially appealing when there isn't much to be gained from making a change. In that scenario, it's difficult to justify the effort when the outcome isn't all that significant. In fact, many people are able to find peace simply by doing nothing.

Two, we can do nothing and yet continue to wish things were different. People who "wish" things instead of taking action often complain about what *is* and find external factors to blame for their circumstances. For obvious reasons, this option can lead to frustration and disappointment. And it certainly won't change the circumstances.

Or three, we can create deliberate, clear goals and take action to change our reality. This option provides us with the greatest opportunity for finding meaning and happiness. But, of the three, it's also the option that requires the most effort (though "wishing" also requires a certain amount of time and energy.)

Even when we have a deep desire to change, creating that change can be a challenge. We have a tendency to cling to familiarity and predictability. Doing nothing is much easier. We repeat past behaviors because it requires less effort than trying new things. In fact, we resist almost all types of change—even when the change has the potential to improve our life. How many times have you considered joining a gym, but never got around to actually signing up for a membership? How often have you talked about starting your own business, but still find yourself sitting in your familiar cubicle every week? We turn down job opportunities, complain about office politics and stay in dysfunctional relationships because the unknown is somehow scarier than our miserable reality.

As a health coach, I saw this form of paralysis a lot, even when it involved some of the simplest changes. Often just cracking the door on the *idea* of change was enough to send people into a state of panic. I've learned that we have to step toward change on our own terms, when we are ready. We have to open the door to change ourselves. If we aren't ready, no amount of encouragement or prodding will be effective, at least not in the long-term.

Although most of us understand that our intentions are useless without action, many of us continue to be ambivalent about changing our safe behaviors, even when we know that health improvements would likely follow. Coaching can be particularly helpful when we feel lost or stuck in a state of inaction.

Dr. Michael Arloski (2007), author of *Wellness Coaching for Lasting Lifestyle Change*, points out that all change creates loss, even when the benefits of change are overwhelmingly positive. Letting go of what is familiar to us can be difficult to accept. In fact, research has shown that we give more attention to negative outcomes, when there is a risk that we may lose something rather than when we stand to gain

event or simply taking a walk outside. One huge benefit of choosing healthy activities for play is that they can also help support other self-care goals as well.

IN PRACTICE

What, Why, How, Do It Now!

What specifically about your luminescent health needs the most attention? For example: authenticity, self-acceptance, embracing imperfections, spending time in meditation, studying yoga, exploring your faith or spiritual beliefs, becoming self-aware, etc.

Why is this specific area of your luminessence important to you right now? Are there significant consequences at stake if you do not address your concerns? Would an improvement in this area of your health allow you to live with more meaning and purpose?

How could you further develop your luminessence? Try to come up with at least three ideas.

Do It Now! Take one step right now... even if it's small: schedule time for stillness, set your alarm for quiet time, take a "well" day or vacation, attend a retreat, work with a life coach, write a reminder on a post-it note, call a friend to ask for their support, etc.

CHAPTER 4: FINANCIAL HEALTH

Financial health is often overlooked when it comes to self-care, but left unmonitored it can be a major source of stress, which can seriously impair our ability to achieve goals. How we allocate our resources, no matter how scarce or plentiful they may be, can either add to or relieve stress. Being in financial harmony means that we are better suited to meet our basic needs as well as achieve our goals.

This dimension of self-care was a critical factor in my decision to take time off. Because I had carefully planned my finances in advance, I had the flexibility and freedom to make bold decisions about my life. In that regard, how we allocate our resources can be a significant determinant of our overall health.

The primary self-care practices that influence our financial health are:

Assessing Needs
Defining Enough
Spending
Saving
Downsizing

ASSESSING NEEDS

We often confuse needs with wants because our materialistic culture has made it hard to tell the difference. Instead of buying healthy food or saving money, we use our expendable income (or credit) to buy the latest gadgets, trendy clothes and fancy cars. And when we compare what we have with what we actually need, this truth becomes even more evident.

Abraham Maslow's hierarchy of needs serves as a visual guide for understanding how our needs are ordered. The pyramid-shaped model suggests that certain needs must be met before we can reach the apex, what Maslow refers to as self-actualization. Many of our needs (physiological, safety, love and belonging and self-esteem) are prerequisites for this higher level.

At the bottom of the pyramid, we find the most basic needs for human survival. Physiological requirements like food, water, oxygen, clothing, shelter and sleep are essential to support life. Without them we can't focus on meeting needs in other areas.

The next category is safety, which includes other necessities such as transportation, employment, and insurance. Health is viewed here as a resource because it enables (or impedes) our ability to access additional resources to meet other needs.

The need for love and belonging is typically filled by our family, friends and community. When we feel accepted and supported, we're able to build the confidence and courage to pursue our goals. And when

living our purpose is that most of us are so caught up in day to day life that we don't give much thought to our desires beyond what we need at the moment. For me, it took leaving a corporate job to explore the possibilities.

Mark Twain said it best. "Twenty years from now you will be more disappointed by the things that you didn't do than by the ones you did." Take risks. Be fearless. Believe in yourself. Pursue your dreams. If others want to come along with you, great. If not, you'll still be living your purpose.

As the title of this book implies, *upward* is a directional movement, not a destination. It's the journey toward *living* our inner truth—*living* our purpose.

TAKING RISKS

Fear is our biggest enemy. As human beings who value safety and survival, we don't like to take risks. But taking calculated risks is essential for moving us forward.

When I was six, my mother packed up our belongings and moved us from Ohio to Florida. That decision, which was an especially radical move at the time—shaped my entire life. I'm not sure I even realized how scared she was. We couldn't afford to stay at a hotel (I know because we stopped at several to check prices), so she ended up driving through the night. That move forced me to change my circle of friends, my cultural norms, my school and all of my familiar routines. But it also opened new opportunities and exposed me to new things. I saw proof that the world was full of possibilities beyond those available in my small town. Sometimes we have to trust our heart and trust the journey. My mother knew it, and now I do too.

Fear can be paralyzing. It keeps us in jobs, relationships and communities that are familiar to us because predictability brings us a false sense of safety. While these circumstances may feel safe, they aren't always healthy. Abusive relationships might be predictable, but they are equally destructive. Repetitive jobs may pay the bills, but they don't necessarily allow us to share our true gifts with the world. Fear limits our ability to express our inner selves completely, and to enjoy some of life's more rewarding experiences. Worrying doesn't change our reality. (I know because I've tried.)

Eleanor Roosevelt is known for her many inspiring quotes. One of my favorites is this: "Do the things that interest you and do them with all your heart. Don't be concerned about whether people are watching or criticizing you. Chances are they aren't paying attention to you." It's true. They probably aren't. And even if they are, something or someone else will steal their attention soon enough.

"What do you *do*?" This question almost always makes its way into even the most casual social conversations. What we "do" is how we define each other. Most of us do something to earn a paycheck, but when that something no longer aligns with our unique skills, we begin to resent what we do. The moment we decide to make a change, we are taking a risk. There are many levels of risk, of course, but making any change involves some risk. If you feel apprehensive about your current life trajectory, then it's worth at least considering a change.

Loving what we do is a combination—a delicate balance, really—of choosing something we love and choosing to love what we do. Some days the latter task is easier than others. But the only person who has the authority to make tough decisions about your life is you. You are the CEO, which also means you're responsible for your own success. (Fortunately, you also get to decide what success looks like.)

If you're like most people, when you think about change you probably think about BIG changes. And that often leads to endless objections about why change isn't possible. Perhaps you have family responsibilities, financial struggles or legal issues that are limiting your options. Or maybe you feel that you lack the knowledge and education to make a change. That may be true in some cases, but remember that change doesn't necessarily have to be monumental. You may not need to leave your job. Perhaps you simply need to change your perspective about the job you have. Change doesn't have to be dramatic to make life more enjoyable.

Each of us has the ability to change something, but we have to be willing to invest our time and energy for that change occur. Intentions are nothing without action. Even if you choose to change nothing, you've still made a choice.

When I decided to take a year off, I knew I was taking a risk. There were no guarantees. (A year later, there still aren't any.) We could have easily experienced a change in circumstances—financial or otherwise—that could have forced me go back to work earlier than planned. And even if that were the case, there were no guarantees that I would have been able to find a job within my field, or at a salary that was comparable to the one I left. When I made the decision to take time off, I had no magic formula or predictive analysis to assure me that everything would be okay. Yet I knew everything would be okay. Why? Because I did my best to plan ahead for my journey, I was mentally tough enough to take the risk and I was resilient enough to change my plan if and when I needed to.

To explore life's possibilities and experience them fully, we have to take risks, but it's up to us to determine what level of risk we are comfortable with.

TAKING PERSONAL RESPONSIBILITY

Each of us is responsible for our own actions—or lack of action, as the case may be. No one likes to fail, but we have no problem basking in the glow of recognition for things we've done well.

When I was nine, my mother tired of hearing me complain about having to wear my seatbelt, so she suggested I write a letter to the President. I'd be lying if I said I wasn't disappointed that Ronald Reagan didn't answer my letter personally, but I did receive some stickers and a letter from the U.S. Department of Transportation outlining the importance of safety belts to public safety. The experience made me feel validated somehow. I learned that I could voice my opinion even if others might not agree with me. I learned that life isn't something that just happens to us, it's something we can participate in.

Most of us don't like the idea of taking personal responsibility. We don't like being blamed when things go wrong, and we certainly don't like to think we somehow contributed to a problem. It's much easier to point a finger and blame something or someone else. External factors are an easier target.

Looking back on my life, I certainly haven't always made the best choices. Many of my decisions were met with consequences that I hadn't fully considered. Regardless, I must accept responsibility for them, learn from them and move forward.

To live our purpose, we must take responsibility for all of our life choices—both the good and the not-so-good ones. While we certainly can't control every aspect of our circumstances, we can change how we respond to those circumstances. We can't control where we are born, the belief systems we are born into or the families that raise us any more than we can control genetic anomalies or physical limitations. But even so, we have the ability to make our reality better in some way.

IN PRACTICE

What, Why, How, Do It Now!

What specifically about your aptitudinal health needs the most attention? For example: discovering your strengths, cultivating your unique skills and talents, learning something new, taking a class, making a career change, etc.

Why is this specific area of your aptitudinal health important to you right now? Are there significant consequences at stake if you do not address your concerns? Would an improvement in this area of your health allow you to achieve?

How could you improve your aptitudinal health? Try to come up with at least three ideas.

Do It Now! Take one step right now... even if it's small: attend a workshop, schedule an appointment with a life coach, apply for a new job, update your resume, taking a quiz to determine your strengths, etc.

CHAPTER 7: RELATIONAL HEALTH

RELATIONSHIP: HOW WE CONNECT WITH OTHERS

Humans have a fundamental need to connect with other living things. Even those who prefer extended periods of alone time still have a need for some amount of connection.

The primary self-care practices that influence our relational health are:

Connecting
Guarding Your Inner Circle
Creating Meaningful Relationships
Loving Others
Setting Boundaries

CONNECTING

Like communication, which relates to the emotive dimension of self-care, connecting with others is central to our relational health. In *Lean In*, Sheryl Sandberg (2013) reminds us that no one accomplishes anything alone. We cannot achieve greatness on our own because living isn't a solo gig. As human beings, we make connections. It's what we do.

In recent years, we've become used to invisible connections found on social media platforms. We connect this way because we're convinced it's more efficient, faster and convenient, allowing us to connect anywhere, anytime.

Having positive connections does really matter. According to Caroline Adams Miller, those who are the happiest have vibrant social circles. Interestingly, strong optimists tend to have greater social support than pessimists (perhaps it's because they also tend to work harder at relationships) and, interestingly, the flipside is also true. Having strong social networks enhances optimism. In other words, nurturing our connections sets us up to experience more optimism.

But not everyone needs to feel the same level of connection. Some people require more time alone, while others need to be surrounded with high levels of energy. While there are certainly people who fall somewhere in the middle, introverts typically require far less socialization than extroverts (Cain, 2012).

Introverts prefer to spend more time in quiet reflection. Uncomfortable group dynamics can make them feel anxious, partly because they are in tune with the emotions of others and partly because they need time to process their own ideas and thoughts in private. Overstimulation does not provide them that space. I can relate. I value my quiet time, perhaps partly because I'm an only child. While I almost always enjoy interacting with groups of people, long periods of social interactions leave me feeling physically and emotionally exhausted. I've found that I need equal parts quiet and connection to feel balanced. Not having siblings has probably also contributed to the fact that I've always had relatively small inner circles. I'm most comfortable being alone or with small groups.

In contrast, some people feel more balanced when they are surrounded by other people. As you might suspect, many extroverts find it extremely uncomfortable to be alone in quiet. More stimulation is needed for them to reach what Cain calls the "sweet spot."

It's important to realize that each of us has a different requirement when it comes to socialization and connecting, and knowing this can help us better understand ourselves and those around us.

GUARDING YOUR INNER CIRCLE

Our friends are our trusted advisors. Those who we consider part of our "inner circle" are people we confide in and seek advice from, which is why we must choose them carefully.

In high school I discovered that a friend of mine was a habitual shoplifter. I was surprised, to say the least, because she and I had gone on several shopping excursions together, but I had never seen her actually steal anything. One day, I heard her bragging to a group of friends about the things she had taken, and I was shocked. (I had been with her!) I confronted her and I remember feeling angry and betrayed that she would place me in a situation where it would seem that I was also involved. I immediately set a boundary that ultimately ended our shopping relationship. It wasn't that I didn't like her as a person. In fact, there were many qualities about her that I both loved and admired. I simply wasn't willing compromise my personal values to maintain the relationship.

The unavoidable truth is that we become like those we spend time with. We pick up their traits and mannerisms, repeat things we've heard them say and, sometimes, even begin to blend their values and beliefs with our own. Most of the time we don't even realize it's happening.

Dr. Nicholas Christakis studied how our relationships impact our health, and it turns out they can be either positive—or, in some cases, even harmful. He explains that "…we adopt the attitudes of the people with whom we live, work, play, and socialize." And our behaviors tend to mirror them as well. If our friends are smokers, our chance of being a smoker increases. If our friends are overweight or obese, our risk for being overweight or obese also increases.

There may be times where we find that we need to usher out some of our inner circle members—not because they are bad people, but because life circumstances transform the relationship to the point that it's no longer mutually beneficial. If members of your inner circle make you feel anxious or uncomfortable, or pressure you to engage in activities that don't align with your personal values, then it may be time to reevaluate the relationship.

Examine your words and mannerisms closely. Chances are you've picked up some habits from your inner circle. Are your trusted advisors making your life richer, or are they preventing you from achieving your goals or being true to yourself? Are you behaving in a way that reflects your luminessence? If not, it may be time for an adjustment.

Although this may be true, it doesn't mean that we should ditch our friends at the first sign of a disagreement. Even the best of friends disagree. A heartfelt conversation about the situation may be all that's needed, but sometimes we need to set boundaries, placing limits on when, where and how often we interact with them.

Of course, maintaining a circle of friends who are exactly like us does have some drawbacks as well. For one, it limits our potential for personal growth, because it's unlikely that we'll be challenged to think differently. Friends who are like us also think like us, which means they share many of our opinions and mostly reinforce our beliefs. This failure to consider other perspectives can be a detriment when it comes to creative problem-solving.

But, ultimately, we must decide for ourselves whether these "other perspectives" are sensible. It's one thing to be open to a new perspective on eating habits, and another thing entirely to consider breaking the law. In the example above, I could have chosen instead to remain "open" to the idea that shoplifting was an acceptable behavior. But that would have been in direct conflict with my core values.

By the same token, it can be downright exhausting to spend extended periods of time with people whose beliefs and personal goals are in direct conflict with our own. This is especially frustrating when the beliefs are deeply entrenched to the point that neither party is willing to consider alternative perspectives. Disagreeing is one thing, but *how* we disagree is what matters.

Abraham Lincoln once selected a team of his biggest adversaries—some would even say his enemies—to serve in his cabinet of trusted advisors. He understood the value of having his opinions challenged. By welcoming the thoughts and ideas of those who fundamentally disagreed with him, he was able to carefully consider all sides of problems. Again, we can choose not only *who* we spend time with, but we can also choose the circumstances as well.

So how do we determine who should be part of our inner circle? One easy question to ask is whether the person fills your cup or drains it. (And an equally important question, do you fill *their* cup or drain it?) Are they always complaining or do they provide encouragement and support as well? Are they someone you could call at 2 AM if you needed help? Is the relationship mutually beneficial? If so, they may be an inner circle prospect.

The size of our inner circle isn't as important as the quality of connections within it. Some people are continuously adding new members to their inner circle. Those with wide social networks are often more outgoing and spend more time participating with groups, and those who are more introverted tend to keep their circles small.

Additionally, it's up to each of us to decide how close we become with our circle-mates, and how much time we are willing to spend nurturing those relationships. Just because someone has a large circle, doesn't mean the relationships are intimate. Regardless of the size of your circle, the important thing is that we connect with others in a way that fosters positive relationships.

Our relationships drive our behaviors too. Research has shown that healthy behaviors are contagious. Whether you refer to it as "group-think" or "social norms," these comfortable and acceptable behaviors within our core groups can influence our decisions. In some circles, profanity is acceptable; in others it's offensive. The longer we interact with individuals or groups of people, the more we pick up their behaviors. If they are healthy ones, we benefit. If they are unhealthy, we often lose. That's why so many weight loss programs encourage forming a support system or selecting an accountability partner early on. The likelihood that we will accomplish our goals is much greater when we have constant encouragement to help us stay on track. Whether we know it or not, we choose what we see frequently. (Ever wonder why certain products are placed at eye level at the supermarket? We see; we buy. It's that simple.) The same holds true for our behaviors. We see, we do.

People are a lot like chickens. In most social circles there is a pecking order, and when the dynamics of the flock changes (think organizational change) the pecking order changes too. Likewise, we tend to go along with what the rest of the flock is doing—at least, unless we fundamentally disagree with something.

Whomever you choose to be part of your inner circle, choose wisely.

CREATING MEANINGFUL RELATIONSHIPS

Meaningful relationships are mutually beneficial. When we meet people who share similar interests and goals, we propel each other toward success. The opposite is also true.

Simply put, relationships are the connections we form with other people. Many of our strongest connections are built and nurtured without the need for an agenda. They simply bring us a sense of joy.

All relationships—regardless if they are inner or outer circle connections—offer us some level of support, even if that support happens to be virtual. Business relationships support our career, community relationships support our need for belonging and contribution and personal relationships support our need for love and support. It's been said that people come into our lives for a reason, a season or a lifetime. Some people fill our cup once, some empty it, and others keep refilling it over the course of our lives. Meaningful relationships—the ones we value and cherish—require more. It takes effort to keep a cup full.

I've been writing to my high school chemistry teacher for over 20 years now. Every once in a while, special people enter our lives. They encourage us, mentor us and support us in ways they sometimes don't even realize. This teacher reminded me that even the most complicated problems have solutions—and that the process of solving them can be fun! Every year, we exchange Christmas cards and a few brief highlights of our life's adventures. I look forward to hearing from her each year and I'm so grateful for the positive impact she has had on my life.

Creating meaningful relationships requires a certain level of empathy, the ability to step into someone else's shoes to understand their unique experiences with life. A coaching client of mine once shared an inspiring story about his weight loss journey. It began with a life-changing event that caused him to drift into unhealthy behaviors that eventually led him to gain a significant amount of weight. At some point, he decided that he would join a cycling group, something he had enjoyed in the past. No doubt, it was much more challenging after he'd gained the weight. But he was determined. At first, he was almost always the last cyclist to finish, but as time went on he began to improve—and he also began to lose weight. Eventually, he was able to keep up with some of the front runners in the group, which didn't go unnoticed. A fellow cyclist asked him about his dramatic improvement, and he decided to prove a point. To illustrate his journey, he convinced this cyclist to tie several extra pounds of sand bags to his bike to experience what is was like to ride with extra weight. My client explained how powerful that demonstration was for both of them. His cycling friend had no idea how challenging it had been, and my client had no idea that his friend was so unaware. When we invest in understanding how life is different for those around us, we can begin to create meaningful connections.

LOVING OTHERS

Martin Luther King, Jr.'s *Strength to Love* is one of my favorite books. Along with other resilient optimists like Viktor Frankl, King has the amazing ability to see goodness through suffering. His hopefulness about the future is infectious, and his ability to see the long-term consequences of our attitudes and actions makes his writing powerful still today.

When we *choose* to love others, we also willingly place ourselves at risk for being disappointed. But loving others in spite of their imperfections is what loving is all about.

Love is also a form of communication. In his book, *The Five Love Languages*, Gary Chapman (1995) explains how Touch, Quality Time, Acts of Service, Words of Affirmation and Gifts are unique styles of expressing and receiving love. The notion that each of us possesses a preferred love language makes it easier to understand how there can often be misunderstandings when we interact with someone who uses a different language. If we try to express love by giving a gift to someone who speaks in terms of quality time, we're missing the mark. Loving requires a deep connection and a deep understanding of those we love.

Sometimes loving others also means forgiving them. Just as we learn to embrace our own imperfections, we must also apply this to those we care about. Forgiveness communicates that we don't expect perfection from others any more than we expect it from ourselves. Forgiveness allows all of us to be human beings.

SETTING BOUNDARIES

While forgiveness is a form of love, it doesn't mean that we should let others take advantage of us or harm us with their actions. Setting boundaries isn't just about saying no; it's also about knowing when to say yes.

When we decide how to spend our time or money, we are setting boundaries. A schedule sets boundaries around how we spend our time; a budget sets boundaries around how we spend and save. Likewise, some boundaries involve people. We sever unhealthy relationships, set limits on social commitments and create boundaries around our use of technology. Boundaries help us stay focused on our high-priority areas rather than getting pulled into time-draining activities that don't support our goals or strengths.

Not having enough time to do everything we want to do is a common complaint, though not always a legitimate one. Saying that we don't have enough time is an easy way to avoid taking responsibility for making poor use of our time and resources. We all make time for the things that are important to us—whether it's lounging on the couch and binge watching our favorite TV show or studying for an advanced degree. The choice is ours.

I remember my grandmother used to say she was more productive when she was "busy." Looking back on my own life, I've found the same to be true. The times in my life that have been the most chaotic have also been my most productive times. When you think about it, all we really have is time. And it's how we spend that time that determines what we will experience in life. There is always enough time. Sometimes we just have to rearrange our priorities and responsibilities to make sure we're spending the time we do have wisely.

Overcommitting is one example of how our failure to set boundaries can have a negative impact on our life. Making commitments that extend beyond our abilities not only creates stress, but it also prevents us from making progress on our goals. Setting limits is about knowing when and how to politely decline tasks and activities that don't align with our goals.

Of course there are circumstances where it's difficult, if not impossible, to set boundaries. At work, we have certain obligations that must be carried out if we want to keep our job. But how those tasks are carried out is often negotiable. I've helped employees adjust their work schedules to better fit their personal style and work preferences, and often these improvements in workflow led to higher efficiency and productivity. In that regard, having a meaningful, solution-oriented conversation with your leadership team could dramatically improve your well-being. As caregivers, we also have difficulties setting boundaries. Children, family members and close friends often place demands on us that have a poor impact on our health over time. Having wide support systems helps lighten the load, and learning to ask for help is crucial.

The next time someone asks you to commit to doing something that you don't feel you can adequately manage, consider responding with something like the following: "That sounds really interesting, but I'm not able to commit to that right now. If something similar comes up in the future, I'd love to hear more about it." Being honest about your inability to commit not only prevents your feeling resentful about doing something you don't really want to do, but it also ensures the right person gets selected for the task.

And if you're asked to do something that doesn't align with your current goals at all, consider politely (but honestly) responding with something like: "Wow, that's a really great idea, but it doesn't sound like it fits in with what I'm working on at the moment. Do you know anyone else that might have an interest?" This helps shift the focus to finding a more suitable fit for the project. Just because you say no doesn't mean you can't still be helpful.

Similarly, it's also okay to respond with something like, "Let me give it some thought and get back to you," rather than immediately committing. Taking adequate time to consider whether we want to invest our time in something is vital. Ultimately, what we should be asking ourselves is, "Does this project make the best use of *me*?"

My inner voice—or "intuition"—has proven to be my best filter when it comes to setting boundaries. If I hear my inner voice shouting, "Noooo! That sounds terrible! Don't do it!" then it's a good indication I need to say, "No, but thank you."

The unpleasant reality is that saying "no" sometimes makes us unpopular. Some people hear the word "no" and view it as a personal affront or a form of rejection; that's just something that goes with the territory. It's important to keep in mind, too, that doing a job half-assed hurts both parties. And being true to yourself (and your purpose) is much more satisfying than pleasing other people. There are polite ways to say no.

As we discussed earlier in the chapter on emotive health, sometimes boundaries need to be set around technology as well. While it may make us more productive in some regards, technology doesn't always have a positive impact, especially when it comes to our relationships. Arguments ignite more rapidly on social media platforms because our messages lack voice intonation and body language that also conveys meaning. It's also much easier to be unkind while hiding behind a keyboard where we cannot see the effects of our comments on others. (And some people just like to stir the pot.) Setting boundaries around how we interact with others using technology can also create healthy boundaries.

Our affinity for virtual connections does have drawbacks. While some researchers are cautious to use the term "addiction," it's clear the over-use of technology is becoming a problem. Even if there are no immediate, measurable effects, it certainly doesn't go unnoticed. Trying to talk to someone who is clearly distracted by engaging Facebook posts sends a message that your relationship isn't important. Sometimes we just have to unplug.

As an experiment, I decided to take a one-year hiatus from Facebook. What made me decide to cut the cord? First, I was fairly certain it would be really hard to do since I felt attached to it. And second, it had become a source of negativity for me. Not only was I checking my news feeds constantly, which consumed more of my time than I cared to admit, much of what I read there was a never-ending list of complaints, unkind comments and "look at me" posts. If I had to guess, I was only interacting regularly with 20% of those on my friends list, and I wanted to develop a deeper connection with the people I cared about. I was tired of being an observer, so I deleted my account.

I replaced my *virtual* friends list with an old-fashioned index card system that I've used for years to organize my contacts. I thought if I took the time to put pen to paper, the quality of the interactions would somehow improve. The results surprised me. While I'm really glad I did it, shunning membership in the most active online network presented a number of challenges.

First, hand-written letters and phone calls aren't exactly mainstream these days. (For those who aren't familiar, phones are devices that allow you to use your voice to communicate.) Ironically, most of the replies to my letters came in the form of an email or text. Though the responses were overwhelmingly positive, it was clear that reading and writing words on paper was not a normal experience. (Honestly, it was even a challenge to find stationery.) Snail mail communication just isn't as popular anymore. I also found that, on average, it took two hand-written letters to receive one hand-written response (or email). Perhaps the second letter guilted them into a response. I'm not sure why I was so surprised by this, but I eventually realized that I'm the abnormal one.

I've always been a letter-writer. Growing up, my parents lived in different states so I spent half of each year writing to distant friends. Today, we have more convenient options to exchange ideas and information. It's much faster. (Everything is much faster.)

Being disconnected from Facebook also left me disconnected from my real community. Many businesses today use Facebook as their primary marketing tool, which meant in some cases I couldn't even find details about hours or locations easily. Not being a member left me isolated.

My biggest take-away from that experience was the realization that the depth of our relationships depend on our willingness to devote time to them. It doesn't really matter if the connection is virtual or not. What matters is the effort we put into those relationships. I also realized that setting boundaries can be as simple as adjusting what comes into my news feed.

It's clear that we are able to form bonds in many ways, but the most meaningful connections require more effort than punching buttons on a keyboard. Taking a break from technology periodically is a good practice because it forces us to connect with others in a more meaningful way.

IN PRACTICE

What, Why, How, Do It Now!

What specifically about your relational health needs the most attention? For example: setting boundaries, setting limits on technology, loving others, etc.

Why is this specific area of your relational health important to you right now? Are there significant consequences at stake if you do not address your concerns? Would an improvement in this area of your health allow you create connections that have more meaning and depth?

How could you improve your relational health? Try to come up with at least three ideas.

Do It Now! Take one step right now... even if it's small: journal ideas for telling someone "no" in a kind way, reduce the time you spend with people who don't align with your luminessence, deactivate one or more of your social media accounts, set limits on the frequency and amount of time you spend with social media, send letters or messages to connections you haven't nurtured in a while, make plans to spend time with someone you love, etc.

CHAPTER 8: ENVIRONMENTAL HEALTH

ENVIRONMENT: HOW WE HARMONIZE WITH NATURE

We experience our environment in several different ways. On a global scale, we interact with the natural world as part of a larger ecosystem—the earth and all of its living things. But on a smaller scale, we interact with our surroundings in the personal spaces we occupy—at home, at work, and in our community. When we are in harmony with our environments, we feel balanced and energized. When we are not, we feel stress and discord.

The primary self-care practices that influence our relational health are:

Learning from Nature
Creating Inspiring Spaces

LEARNING FROM NATURE

Growing up on my family's small farm in Ohio, I learned a lot by observing nature. I was chased by a duck and learned that animals are very protective of their young. I learned that horses are beautiful, but they are also very smart and can instantly recognize a chump (me). I learned that if you fall asleep in the grass, your pet turtle will (slowly) walk away. I learned that you should never cut a bale of hay with the pocket-knife's blade pointing toward you (because that is how "One-eyed Joe" earned his nickname). And I also learned that you cannot effectively catch a rabbit by throwing a blanket over it.

Sometimes, though, nature's lessons are much bigger. When I was five I took an apple from our neighbor's tree without asking and ended up in the emergency room. As it turns out, I am highly allergic to yellow jacket stings, and I learned in a matter of minutes how scary anaphylaxis can be. In addition to learning about my allergy, I also learned that taking something without asking has consequences.

Spending time in nature has a way of centering us. It reminds us that we are part of something bigger. Whether we're hiking or camping or simply sitting outside, peace lives within the trees.

Our relationship with nature is symbiotic—living things support other living things. Life is interconnected. When we consider the many connections (root systems between plants, fungi in the soil and relationships between people) it's pretty amazing really. But most of us are too distracted to venture outside to learn much anymore. We take for granted that life will continue despite our neglect and careless actions.

Every time we fail to look beyond our urban window and choose to pay others to grow our food, we disconnect a little more from our environment. We disconnect from nature when we teach our children that food needs to be perfect, free from blemishes, to be fit to eat. We disconnect from nature when we buy products without giving a thought to the processes used to manufacture and ship them. We disconnect from nature when we throw things "away" without giving a thought to where they go after they leave our curbside bin. We are just one small part of the world's ecosystem, but our daily choices do have a lasting impact on every living thing, our families included.

It's been estimated that we are currently using 1-½ times the ecological resources available on earth to support our population (Vogliano, Brown, Miller, et al., 2015), and it seems our affinity for using credit to pay our debts isn't limited to our finances.

Permaculture, or "permanent agriculture," is an interconnected, multidimensional system of design principles that was first developed in the 70's by Bill Mollison and his student David Holmgren. At its core, permaculture is about recognizing that we have a personal responsibility to care for the earth (Mollison, 1988). The approach itself is rooted in whole-systems thinking, using nature's natural patterns to solve problems and make decisions. What is its overall objective? To create a more sustainable agricultural system—one that produces energy rather than simply devouring it. The philosophy is built around three simple intentions:

Care for the earth
Care for people
Share the surplus

Permaculture also addresses the many connections that exist between living things that share spaces and communities. In fact, some feel that permaculture is better described as "permanent culture." Working *with* nature, permaculture designers learn to "go with the flow" instead of imposing their selfish desires upon a landscape. In this way, permaculture is a tool that can be used to achieve exponentially positive outcomes.

CREATING INSPIRING SPACES

It's important for us to feel good in the spaces that we spend the majority of our time. The demands of life can be overwhelming, and retreating to zones that boost our spirits can help us recharge and rebalance. Eliminating clutter is one way to create more harmony in our personal spaces. As pointed out earlier, the process of decluttering can also be a catalyst for other changes that have a positive impact on our health. If I had it to do all over again, I would have addressed this dimension much earlier in my sabbatical. Clearing the clutter also clears our mind.

After reading Marie Kondo's book, *The Life-Changing Magic of Tidying Up: The Japanese Art of Decluttering and Organizing*, I spent two weeks sorting, purging, donating and organizing the "things" I have accumulated over the past 38 years. Kondo's simple solution is this: examine each item that you own and decide first *if* you want to keep it and *where* to put it if you do (Kondo & Hirano, 2014). She reminds us that letting go of things in our life is more important than adding them. And although I hadn't realized it before, she is right about why we have trouble letting go. It's usually either because we have an attachment to the past or a fear of the future. Decluttering is a great first step for creating inner peace. Clearing the chaos and distractions from our personal spaces gives us room to develop a vibrant vision of our future.

It was much simpler than I imagined it would be, though I quickly realized I would need to repeat the same process again if I really wanted to whittle my belongings down to the bare necessities. A single pass simply would not be enough. It was slightly embarrassing to find that I had duplicates of a few things, which also meant that I had so much stuff that prior purchases were buried beneath more recent ones.

How we feel at home and at work really does make a difference. Feeling relaxed, calm, safe and inspired is much more motivating than feeling agitated, anxious, and stressed. If you aren't feeling good in the areas where you spend the majority of your time, it might be necessary to consider making some changes. Changing our environment doesn't have to include a moving truck. By simply altering paint colors, decor, lighting or furniture placement, we can change the look and feel of any room.

IN PRACTICE

What, Why, How, Do It Now!

What specifically about your environmental health needs the most attention? For example: spending time outside, organizing your personal spaces, gardening, etc.

Why is this specific area of your environmental health important to you right now? Are there significant consequences at stake if you do not address your concerns? Would an improvement in your environmental health allow you to feel more connected?

How could you improve your environmental health? Try to come up with at least three ideas.

Do It Now! Take one step right now… even if it's small: drop what you are doing right now and step outside to inhale the air, go for a walk, make your bed, declutter your workspace, etc.

CHAPTER 9: DESIGNING YOUR SELF-CARE PRACTICE

Put simply, a system is a set of connected things. The last eight chapters have explored each of the eight dimensions of self-care individually, and it should be clear that there are many areas of overlap and interconnectedness between them. When each dimension is functioning optimally, we can enjoy greater health benefits and levels of life satisfaction.

A self-care system is an intentional, comprehensive plan that supports all eight of the self-care dimensions. While that may sound daunting at first, it's important to remember that "support" comes in all shapes and sizes. You will likely find that you'll need to put forth greater efforts in some dimensions and less in others.

The design phase is where the real magic happens. Creating a self-care system that reflects your unique values, beliefs, skills and personal goals can be a powerful motivator for living well. Over time, you'll find that it doesn't take as much effort to maintain as it did in the beginning.

One of the most important pieces of developing a self-care plan is to put the plan in writing. Having a clear mental picture of your destination is great, but unless you have a physical map to reference, it's easy to get lost.

In this chapter, we'll take a look at some strategies for designing a personal self-care practice that fits your unique needs. We'll also describe how to construct clear, meaningful goals within each of the dimensions to ensure that your actions generate the greatest results.

Are you ready to live like you mean it? Then, let's get started!

To summarize, the Eight Dimensions of Self-Care are:

SYSTEMIC: How we eat, move and rest
EMOTIONAL: How we express ourselves
LUMINESCENT: How we illuminate our inner truth
FINANCIAL: How we allocate our resources
COGNITIVE: How we think
APTITUDINAL: How we contribute to the world
RELATIONAL: How we connect with others
ENVIRONMENTAL: How we harmonize with nature

CREATING STICKY GOALS

It's important to first understand what makes some goals more achievable than others. How can we put our intentions into words so that we optimize the conditions for achieving them? What exactly makes some goals "stick" and others fade away?

Sticky goals are those goals that draw us in. We can't help but feel excited about them, even though we know they will require a significant amount of our time and energy. These goals aren't easily abandoned with changing life priorities and demands; they are urgent because we place a high value on them. Goals that are sticky usually stem from significant needs in our life rather than fleeting desires. We think about them frequently, and we may even tell others about them. They are the goals that spark an inner desire that pushes us forward toward them.

SMART GOALS

SMART goal-setting has become a highly-popular approach, used in both health-related and organizational environments. Despite its popularity, there is quite a bit of inconsistency with how to best use this method. One reason is that the acronym itself has many interpretations. A quick web search turns up a number of variations, each with its own set of vague descriptions:

S: Specific, Sensible, Significant
M: Measurable, Motivating, Meaningful
A: Actionable, Attainable, Achievable, Assignable
R: Realistic, Relevant, Reasonable
T: Time-bound, Tangible, Truthful, Timely

With that in mind, it's easy to see why goal-setting can be so challenging, especially for those who are new to the process. Of all the variations of SMART goals, I prefer the *Specific, Measurable, Actionable, Realistic* and *Time-Bound* version—but even it presents some practical flaws.

SPECIFIC

Certainly, adding an element of specificity to goals is important. Identifying the who, what, when, and where aspects of a goal help us narrow our focus. Having an intention to "eat healthier" is much less specific than setting a goal of "eating five or more fruits and vegetables every day for the next month." The latter goal gives us a colorful picture of what we exactly want to experience. Meaningful goals must be specific.

MEASURABLE

Goals also need to be measurable. Otherwise, we never know when we've achieved them. By creating clear metrics for measuring goals, we can determine when we've hit our mark. Not having a way to measure our progress over time means we can't effectively make corrections when we discover what we're doing isn't working.

ACTIONABLE

Making a goal actionable implies that the goal-setter is responsible for exerting some amount of energy. Goals don't just come to fruition on their own; they require work. An easy way to make a goal actionable is to use strong verbs. *Hire* a personal trainer, *drink* 8-ounces of water, *schedule* an annual physical or *create* a budget—each of these examples includes a verb that denote action.

Realistic

Ensuring that our goals are realistic is important too. One way to determine if a goal is attainable is to assess our level of confidence. On a scale of 1 to 10 (with 10 being the highest), rate your level of confidence in being able to achieve a goal you've set. If you aren't at least at a 6, then you may want to go back to the drawing board and revise the goal. Sometimes shifting the frequency is all that's needed. For example, a goal of walking for 20 minutes just three days each week may be more realistic than walking all seven, depending on your own personal circumstances.

Time-Bound

Ensuring that goals are time-bound is also critical. Creating a sense of urgency moves us to action and helps us stay motivated to continue moving forward. End dates tell us when to stop and reassess.

But even if you select a version of the SMART goal approach that makes the most sense to you, you'll still be faced with filling in a few missing pieces. One common pitfall with goal-setting is failing to ensure that you actually have the authority to implement and achieve the goal. If your goal is contingent upon others supporting you or influencing the conditions for your success, you may be sorely disappointed with the outcome.

Likewise, to keep motivation high, it's important to connect your *what* to your *why*. Wanting to lose weight is a transient desire unless it's paired with a compelling reason. I once had a client whose primary motivation for losing weight was sky diving. His current weight put him above the limit for safety harnesses, which prevented him from enjoying something he loved. His desire to go sky diving is what propelled him forward. By identifying a clear reason *why* we want something, it increases our motivation and makes it more likely that we'll stay focused on achieving it.

WHAT? WHY? HOW? DO IT NOW!

As a health professional, I've been immersed in a number of behavior change methodologies over the years. SMART goal-setting is by far the most popular method, but, then again, there aren't many alternatives. That's why I developed a more practical approach to goal-setting, and I call it the ***What? Why? How? Do It Now!*** method. This simplified approach to goal-setting can be used to create clear, meaningful goals more effectively and efficiently.

Here is the general framework:

> **What** do you want to accomplish?
> **Why** do you want to accomplish it?
> **How** will you accomplish it?
> **Do It Now!** (your deadline)

To form a goal, simply link the segments together: [**What**] to [**Why**] by [**How**] by [**Do It Now!**]

Here are a few examples:
- Attend strength training class twice per week to increase lean body mass by joining [name of gym] by (deadline)
- Save $3,000 to take a vacation next year by saving $250 each month by (deadline)
- Lose 10 pounds to reduce my risk for diabetes by eating 1,500 calories each day by (deadline)

What-Why-How statements are constructed using strong verbs that are, for the most part, positive in nature. Words like "reduce," "decrease" and "lessen" create a sense of loss, which can reduce our motivation to begin working toward them. For that reason, it's best to reserve those terms for the why segments of our goals (the reason behind them). Reducing cholesterol, decreasing blood pressure and reducing or eliminating the need for medications are all positive reasons that are motivating. Here is a list of 100 verbs to help get you started:

Accumulate	Choose	Cultivate
Attend	Climb	Dance
Be	Communicate	Decrease
Become	Cook	Design
Begin	Coordinate	Develop
Breathe	Complete	Donate
Build	Compose	Double
Buy	Connect	Draft
Celebrate	Create	Drink

Earn	Lessen	Save
Eat	Listen	Schedule
Enhance	Live	See
Enroll	Make	Sell
Establish	Master	Select
Experience	Mediate	Share
Explore	Meet	Sleep
Find	Move	Spend
Finish	Obtain	Strengthen
Form	Organize	Support
Generate	Own	Swap
Get	Participate	Swim
Give	Plan	Take
Graduate	Plant	Teach
Grow	Prevent	Trade
Have	Produce	Travel
Help	Provide	Verbalize
Host	Publish	Visit
Improve	Read	Visualize
Increase	Record	Volunteer
Intensify	Reduce	Watch
Join	Remodel	Win
Laugh	Rest	Write
Launch	Relax	
Learn	Run	

Once you begin, you may find that creating goals is actually quite fun. As the creative ideas start to flow, you'll likely end up with several goals to consider, and the challenge will then be to narrow them down to a subset of goals you can tackle in a realistic time-frame. You may find that you're able to come up with several *why's* and *how's* for each *what*. That's a good thing! The more *why's* you have, the stronger your motivation will be; and the more *how's* you have, the more impact your efforts will have. After you've selected your target goals, simply set a deadline for each one and get to work. Now, let's explore each of the components in more detail.

WHAT

To set meaningful goals, you'll first need to have a clear picture of *what* you want to *have*, *do* or *be*. Next, compare that picture to your current needs and life circumstances to honestly assess what you are ready, willing and able to take on. In your mind, explore *what* you want your life to be like in a month, three months, six months, a year or five years from now. Perhaps your *what* is to climb Mount Everest, to become a doctor, to travel the world or simply to achieve a healthy weight. Your *what* is that thing you crave with an absolute passion. I once had a client whose goal was simply to be at a weight that had a "1" in front of it (her current weight was above 200). This simple goal gave her something to work toward without placing too much pressure on herself.

Close your eyes... can you see your ideal future? What is it that you want? Your most meaningful *what* may be the recurring thoughts that occupy the back of your mind, not yet fully defined. As your *what* develops into a clearer image, you can either find ways to weave it into an existing goal, or simply create a new one.

At this point, it may also be helpful to view your *what* as an "intention" rather than a concrete requirement. Remember that you can change your focus at any time. Life changes whether we like it or not, and the best we can do is to adapt and continue moving forward. As you begin to draft a few *What-Why-How* statements, you'll see that there are infinite ways to achieve your *what*—but only a handful of them will be ones that spark excitement within you. Pay attention to those ones.

WHY

Your *why* is your motivator. It's the reason behind your *what*. Ultimately, it's what fuels your efforts to actively work toward—and to continue working toward—your goals. As you explore your *why*'s, think about what makes your goal important. Why is it so appealing—and why is it a priority for you right now? How do you imagine you will feel after you've accomplished your goal? How will your life be better as a result? The stronger the connection between your *what* and your *why*, the more powerful your desire will be to exert the effort necessary to achieve the goal.

HOW

Your *how* is your strategy for achieving what you desire. List as many possibilities as you can (whether they are realistic or not isn't important right now). Brainstorming without regard to feasibility can bring forward new, creative ideas and solutions. The more ideas you can generate at this stage, the better. Write down EVERY idea you have—even the crazy ones.

Consider also the resources you may need to achieve the goal. Will your goal require funding? Who might be able to help support you? How much time will you need to achieve your goal? As you consider possible goals, think about what you would like to be, improve, increase, have, join, create, begin, develop or learn. Review the list of verbs above for more ideas and remember, the majority of our limitations come from our own self-defeating thoughts.

Here are a few more examples:

Systemic Health:
- Improve cardiovascular fitness to reduce the risk of developing diabetes by walking for 60 minutes, three or more days each week by (deadline).
- Summit Mount Everest to check an item off my bucket list by creating a training schedule by (deadline).

Emotive Health:

- Improve communication skills to be more effective at work by practicing a new skill each time I talk with co-workers by (deadline).

Luminescent Health:
- Be authentic to live in congruence with my purpose by speaking openly about my goals with others by (deadline).

Financial Health:
- Establish a savings plan to fund my son or daughter's college education by scheduling an appointment with a financial advisor by (deadline).
- Pay off debts to begin contributing to a retirement fund by creating and following a monthly budget by (deadline).

Cognitive Health:
- Begin a meditation practice to manage stress by sitting in stillness for 20 minutes each morning by (deadline).

Aptitudinal Health:
- Improve my writing skills to publish a book by enrolling in a writing class by (deadline).
- Identify my personal strengths and skills to increase my self-confidence by completing the VIA signature strengths assessment by (deadline).

Relational Health:
- Establish weekly date nights to develop a deeper connection with my partner by making special dinner reservations every other week by (deadline).

Environmental Health:
- Grow more of my own food to provide nutritious food for my family by planting lettuces and greens by (deadline).

Choose your terminology wisely and make sure the language you use is inspiring and motivating for you personally. Subtle word variations can be powerful motivators (or demotivators). You may also notice that some of your goals could fit into several dimensions. Those are what I call "sweet goals" because they are wide-reaching and efficient when it comes to using our precious time and energy. There is no right or wrong with how you construct your goals. As long as they make sense to you, they are exactly as they should be.

Keep the image of your *what* clear in your mind and imagine the fastest possible way to get there. Then put it in writing. Brian Tracy (2011), author of *No Excuses! The Power of Self-Discipline*, believes that writing out our goals increases the likelihood that we'll achieve them by ten times (or 1,000 percent)!

DO IT NOW!

And finally, perhaps the most important step when it comes to behavior change is to *do it now*! Intentions are useless without action. Knowing, thinking, talking about and analyzing our goals is not doing them. If we truly expect to change the course of our lives, and ultimately live our purpose, then we must be willing to move beyond our intentions, roll up our sleeves and get to work. This last step is without a doubt the hardest, but it's the one that brings the biggest rewards.

Ideas are just ideas; it takes an incredible amount of emotional and physical energy to see an idea or project through to completion. Merely thinking about the fact that you want to take better care of yourself will do nothing to improve your health. Only your actions, behaviors and habits can do that.

It's no secret that most of us do okay with the *what* and *why* elements of goals, but to successfully achieve them, we must also have a plan (a *how*) and the willingness to take action—the courage to *Do It Now!* Creativity is by far our greatest resource.

Setting a deadline for each goal is critical, even if we later choose to move the target. Goals without deadlines are just wishes.

NARROWING IT DOWN

If you're having trouble determining where to best focus your efforts, it may be helpful to examine each of the eight self-care dimensions in more detail. Narrowing it down to a few areas that would have the greatest impact on your health and your life will help you better identify where to start. The following worksheet represents just one of the ways you might explore some possible goals.

SELF-CARE EXPLORATION WORKSHEET

Systemic			Importance	**Cognitive**			Importance
What	Why	How	Confidence	What	Why	How	Confidence
What	Why	How	Confidence	What	Why	How	Confidence
What	Why	How	Confidence	What	Why	How	Confidence
Emotive			Importance	**Aptitudinal**			Importance
What	Why	How	Confidence	What	Why	How	Confidence
What	Why	How	Confidence	What	Why	How	Confidence
What	Why	How	Confidence	What	Why	How	Confidence
Luminessence			Importance	**Relational**			Importance
What	Why	How	Confidence	What	Why	How	Confidence
What	Why	How	Confidence	What	Why	How	Confidence
What	Why	How	Confidence	What	Why	How	Confidence
Financial			Importance	**Environmental**			Importance
What	Why	How	Confidence	What	Why	How	Confidence
What	Why	How	Confidence	What	Why	How	Confidence
What	Why	How	Confidence	What	Why	How	Confidence

Using a scale of 1 to 10 (with 10 being the highest), rank the importance of each health dimension as it pertains to your life right now. For example, if you feel you have a significant need to improve your Relational health, score it high. But, if you feel that your self-care practices within that dimension are already adequately meeting your needs, score it low. Do this for each of the 8 dimensions. Don't overthink it; go with your gut.

Next, for each dimension write down one to three possible **What-Why-How** statements. Again, using a scale of 1 to 10 (with 10 being the highest), rank your level of confidence in your ability to achieve each of the *What-Why-How* statements you've listed. Don't be surprised if your level of confidence does not match your *perceived* level of importance for the dimension. It's possible that you could recognize a clear need to improve your financial health, but for whatever reason the idea of setting a goal in that category creates stress for you (indicating low confidence). Relax and rank each goal according to how you truly feel about your ability to achieve it—not the way you think you should feel.

After you complete the worksheet, you should have some sense for which of the goals ignited excitement within you, and which ones left you feeling anxious or indifferent. When your importance and confidence rankings are both high, that's a good indication you're on the right track. These goals are probably aligned with your highest priorities. For the goals that you had a positive connection with, brainstorm for more *why*'s and *how*'s. There are many ways to find success.

The next step is to select one to three goals that created the most excitement within you and make a commitment to yourself to get started on them. Don't panic! You can always change, revise or eliminate goals as you move forward. The most important thing is that you have a starting place, and making a commitment to yourself helps push you over the starting line. Give each goal a deadline and get to work!

As you move into the action phase, it can be helpful to share your goals with your support network, as they can provide a great source of encouragement and motivation. Finding others who share your goals can provide an even greater source of motivation.

Every week (yes, every week), assess your progress. One way to do this is to create milestones. If your goal is to lose 20 pounds in six months, that translates to about 1 pound each week to meet that goal. Assessing progress every week helps you identify barriers more quickly. And the earlier you find out an adjustment is needed, the more likely you'll be able to tweak your plan and increase your chances of success.

MOTIVATION AND GRIT

We've all experienced it: that feeling of indifference about our goals. Often, this decline in motivation sets in after just a few weeks of adhering to a plan. We start off feeling energized, inspired and unstoppable, but later lose interest. It can be a vicious cycle. Studies have shown that self-monitoring, like keeping a food diary, is highest in the second week, but declines considerably after about five weeks. Another study showed that changes in schedule, lack of time, forgetting to log, lack of organization, lack of social support and boredom were all found to be factors for failing to self-monitor (Burke, Swigart, Warziski, et al., 2009). While some people achieve their goals without self-monitoring, success is much greater when there is an element of self-awareness that allows for course correction.

We often set audacious goals with every intention of following through with them at the start, but later abandon them because we fall short of our own, often unrealistic, expectations. Having a realistic mindset about the results of our efforts is important too, and that's what makes the process of goal-setting so critical. Here are some tips to help you continue to move forward:

Take at least one action every day that moves you toward one or more of your goals. Start each day by reading through your goals. This simple task helps keep them in the forefront of your mind, enhancing your ability to see potential opportunities to leverage other resources to achieve them throughout the day. Taking at least one action every day ensures that you'll move closer to your target.

Create a positive support network. Surrounding yourself with encouraging, supportive people will help refuel your motivation when you're running low. Finding people who share similar goals can be even more effective because it's equally motivating to help someone else achieve their goals.

Enjoy the small successes. Pursuing your goals should be fun! If it feels like work, perhaps you should loosen your grip a little and adjust your goals so they feel less punitive. Celebrating your successes along the way can help you build confidence and give you the strength to continue your journey.

Stay optimistic. When it comes to goal achievement, it's easy to see why optimists fare better. Research has shown that optimists exert more effort, whereas pessimists disengage from effort. It's not that optimists are more *capable* than pessimists—they're just more persistent. Building optimism may help maintain high levels of motivation.

Our level of motivation is directly tied to our life priorities as well as to our stage of change. Prochaska's Transtheoretcial Stages of Change model lays out five stages of readiness for change: *Precontemplation, Contemplation, Preparation, Action* and *Maintenance*. This model acknowledges that we are in constant state of flux, moving back and forth between the stages on a monthly, weekly, daily and sometimes even hourly basis.

PRECONTEMPLATION

Those who are in the precontemplation stage are not yet ready to make a change. In fact, they probably aren't even considering it yet. Either they do not see a need for change or they are resisting external pressures to change.

CONTEMPLATION

People in the contemplation stage are considering making a change within the next six months, but they are still weighing the pros and cons and aren't quite ready to commit.

PREPARATION

In the preparation stage, plans are being developed and there is an intention to begin making changes within the next month.

ACTION

In the action stage, individuals are engaging in the behaviors they outlined in the preparation stage. They may make revisions to their initial goals along the way, but they are committed to the primary outcomes they want to achieve.

MAINTENANCE

Those in the maintenance stage have been taking action for more than six months, and their primary focus is now on maintaining their new habits and avoiding relapses.

It's important to know that intrinsic motivation is much more powerful than external motivators when it comes to long-term success. All of us have probably been exposed to external motivators at some time in our life. Monetary incentives are popular within corporate wellness programs, and many of them have progressively moved to a more punitive approach, where employees are actually penalized for not taking action. The approaches range from carrots to sticks, and I once heard an executive refer to their program design as a "frozen carrot"—somewhere in between.

But research has shown that financial rewards are not effective in the long-term. External motivators don't last, but when our motivation is internal, coming from within, eventually the behavior becomes part of who we are.

It takes approximately 66 days for a behavior to become a habit (Lally, 2010). It's no surprise, then, why so many people give up before they reach their goals. In *Enthusiasm Makes the Difference* Norman Vincent Peale wrote: "When you have something you believe in, then you can put the amazing power of conviction behind your efforts." He reminds us that the choice lies within us: "...in order to have enthusiasm, simply act enthusiastic."

Other people can be powerful external motivators as well. Sometimes they motivate us by accomplishing things we either fear or feel certain we couldn't do. I was talking with a man recently who had just summited Mount Rainier. This news shocked me because he didn't appear to be in the kind of physical shape I would expect for someone to achieve such a feat. But all I could think about was, *if he can do it, so can I.* While I'm not planning a summit any time soon, it was a moment of realization for me. When we see possibilities through the realities of others, we often find it easier to take on more challenging goals. Watching other people succeed helps us build our own confidence.

Caroline Adams Miller says this about goals: "Set your goals high, work as hard as you can, and then create a positive belief system if you want to create your best life." Having a positive connection with the goals we set for ourselves can dramatically increase our chances of achieving them.

FINDING PROFESSIONAL HELP

It's important to be aware that sometimes life's challenges are too complex to handle alone. Having a strong support network of friends and family is important, but sometimes even that isn't enough. Here are a few examples of a wide variety of professionals who may be able to help you navigate some of the challenges you face with meeting your self-care goals:

REGISTERED DIETITIANS/NUTRITIONISTS

Registered Dietitians (RDs), also known as Registered Dietitian/Nutritionists (RDNs), are the industry's leading nutrition professionals for dietary-related care and treatment. Nutrition counseling has been defined as a process of setting and prioritizing goals, and creating a plan of action that fosters personal responsibility for self-care (Curry & Jaffee, 1997). These professionals can help translate the science of nutrition into practical solutions for preventing and managing specific health conditions. To find a registered dietitian/nutritionist in your area, visit www.eatright.org.

PERSONAL TRAINERS AND EXERCISE SPECIALISTS

Personal trainers and other exercise specialists can be especially helpful to those who are just starting out on their fitness journey. These professionals help develop exercise programs that target specific needs, as well as provide feedback and accountability for achieving the maximal benefits of exercise. Because training and credentials vary greatly among fitness professionals, be

165

sure to ask questions about their education and experience.

PROFESSIONAL COUNSELORS

If you've felt helpless or sad for an extended period of time, find it difficult to handle everyday activities or believe your actions may be harmful to yourself or those around you, talk with your health care provider about how to find a professional counselor therapist. Mental health counselors aren't just for people who suffer from severe mental disorders; they help each of us work through life's ongoing challenges. Likewise, many employee wellness programs also offer free Employee Assistance Programs (EAP) that can connect you with a professional within your network.

FINANCIAL ADVISORS

Some investment firms offer financial advising as part of their bundled services, though many professionals can be hired as independent consultants. Likewise, there are many free online tools and resources that can help you assess and map out a financial plan.

LIFE COACHES

Life coaching has become quite popular over the years as more people explore career alternatives in hopes of finding more fulfilling work. These professionals are trained to ask difficult questions that elicit our internal motivators for change. Since the field of coaching is still mostly unregulated, it's important to review the background and education of potential coaches before selecting one.

PROFESSIONAL ORGANIZERS

Personal organizers help us create spaces that are inspiring and nurturing. Being disorganized creates tension and stress, and having to sort through our chaos means we have less time to spend pursuing goals. Organization experts don't just sort and organize our *things*; they can also help us create peace and harmony in our life.

PERMACULTURE DESIGNERS

Permaculture designers help create inspiring outdoor spaces that use nature as a guide. They thoroughly observe these spaces to determine what is needed, and then arrive at solutions rather than imposing them.

SELF-CARE COACHES

Self-care coaching is a form of health & wellness coaching that focuses on developing a comprehensive self-care practice. This emerging field of health coaching is also gaining popularity within the medical community. Coaches ask insightful questions to help clients verbalize their intentions and eventually translate them into actionable goals. They help clients connect the dots and explore possible solutions to their most challenging roadblocks. But because the industry still lacks standardized education and training, it can be difficult to distinguish experienced coaches from those who have little knowledge or skills. When choosing a coach, be sure to ask questions about their education and experience and assess whether their personality and style is a good match.

CLOSING THOUGHTS

Self-care is taking personal ownership of our health—the systemic, emotive, luminescent, financial, cognitive, aptitudinal, relational and environmental dimensions of our well-being.

When we nurture each dimension of our health, we're fully supported in a way that allows us to live our purpose. That's how we find meaning, happiness, fulfillment and, ultimately, life satisfaction.

Making time to carefully examine each dimension regularly helps ensure that our behaviors match our values, and it also allows us to course correct if we notice that we're out of balance. Giving each dimension the proper attention it deserves can be challenging, but it isn't impossible.

It's easy to blame our individual circumstances—our responsibilities and hardships—for our inability to devote time to self-care. But the reality is that we make time for what is important to us. No matter how much *free* time we have, we can always use that same excuse. People who are retired often find themselves too busy for self-care, and people who take sabbaticals can equally find themselves too busy for self-care. We have a tendency to overcommit our time, no matter how much time we have, and that's why learning to set boundaries is so crucial.

Sabbaticals are not cure-alls. They can't magically fix our problems or fill our life with happiness any more than a weeklong vacation in the Caribbean can. Taking time off doesn't achieve anything in and of itself; it simply gives us the time and space to refocus on what's most important to us. It's how we use the time we have that matters, and once we decide for ourselves what's important, the real work begins.

Furthermore, extended breaks can be counterproductive if we're not careful. Looking back on my sabbatical, it took me six months to truly feel like a whole person again. That's when my body and mind felt adequately rested and re-energized. But while I desperately wanted to re-engage in my life, I still didn't have a clear plan. I soon realized that what I had been seeking all along was a clear vision—a higher purpose that I could pour my heart and soul into. I often wished someone would have asked me the "hard questions" about what I really wanted to do sooner. I realize now that someone should have been a coach. Had I enlisted the help of a professional earlier, I probably would have arrived at my vision much sooner. But using the principles outlined in this book, I eventually redesigned my life to live in congruence with what I believe is my purpose.

If you're feeling even slightly inspired to make some changes in your life, then I hope this book has provided you with a framework for designing a self-care practice that will enable you to refocus your time and energy wisely to fully live your purpose.

What happens next is your choice. You can either continue living out of habit and comfort, or you can dare to explore your heart for the possibilities that still exist within you.

Which will it be?

ABOUT THE AUTHOR

STACY FISHER-GUNN is the founder of Living Upp, a self-care community that empowers people to take personal ownership of their health. She is a Registered Dietitian/Nutritionist (RDN) and Certified Diabetes Educator (CDE) with over 15 years of healthcare experience. Stacy spent many years in the corporate wellness space, working with large companies such as IBM, Dell and The Boeing Company. At WebMD, she served as a health coach and eventually led the company's largest team of on-site coaches—a brilliant group of inspiring individuals. Stacy and her husband, Jeremy, live in Issaquah, Washington with a hilarious group of dogs and chickens.

A Note from the Author

Writing this book has been a labor of love, and I'm fairly certain I could have spent a lifetime refining each sentence, paragraph and chapter to better convey my message. At some point I realized that, while everything we create "could always be better," there comes a time when we must release it into the world in its perfect state of imperfection. Thank you for reading this book, and for taking time to explore how these ideas might apply to your life personally. If you've discovered just one possibility that makes you feel excited, then I have achieved my purpose. I would be grateful if you could take the time to leave me a review on Amazon!

Join Our Community

Living Upp is a self-care community dedicated to empowering individuals to take personal ownership of their health. We invite you to join our community:

Website: www.LivingUpp.com
Facebook: www.Facebook.com/LivingUppdates
Twitter: www.Twitter.com/LivingUppdates

We also love hearing self-care success stories! To share your story, please email Stacy directly at
Stacy@LivingUpp.com.

REFERENCES

Adkins, P.W. (1987). *Molecules*. New York: Times Books.

Ardell, D. B. (1977). High Level Wellness: An Alternative to Doctors, Drugs, and Disease. Emmaus, Penn.: Rodale Press.

Arloski, M. (2007). *Wellness Coaching for Lasting Lifestyle Change*. Duluth, Minn: Whole Person Associates.

Baumeister, R.F., Bratslavsky, E., Finkenauer, C., & Vohs, K.D. (2001). Bad is stronger than good. Review of *General Psychology*. 5(4), 323-370.

Bays, J. (2009). *Mindful Eating*. Boston & London: Shambhala.

Blackwell, S.E., Rius-Ottenheim, N.R., Schulte-van Maaren, W.M., et al. (2013). Optimism and mental imagery: A possible cognitive marker to promote well-being? *Psychiatry Research*, 206:56-61.

Bowen, W. (2007). *A Complaint Free World: How to Stop Complaining and Start Enjoying the Life You Always Wanted*. New York: Doubleday.

Brillat-Savarin, J. A. Fisher, M. F. K. (1971). *The Physiology of Taste: Or, Meditations on Transcendental Gastronomy*. Translated by M. F. K. Fisher. New York: Knopf.

Brown, B. (2010). *The Gifts of Imperfection*. Center City, MN: Hazelden.

Brown, N. J. L., et al. (2013). The complex dynamics of wishful thinking: The critical positivity ratio. *American Psychologist*, 68(9):801-813.

Buettner, D. (2012). *The Blue Zones: 9 Lessons for Living Longer from the People Who've Lived the Longest (2nd Ed.)*. Washington, D.C.: National Geographic.

Burke L.E., Swigart, V., Warziski, T.M., et al. (2009). Experiences of self-monitoring: Successes and struggles during treatment for weight loss. *Qualitative Health Research*, 19(6):815-828.

Cain, S. (2012). *Quiet*. New York: Crown Publishers.

Carver, C.S. and Scheier, M.F. (2014). Dispositional optimism. *Trends in Cognitive Sciences*, 18(6)293-299.

Carver, C.S., Scheier, M.F., & Segerstrom, S.C. (2010). Optimism. *Clinical Psychology Review*, 30, 879-889.

Centers for Disease Control and Prevention (2016, February). "How much physical activity do adults need?" URL: http://www.cdc.gov/physicalactivity/basics/adults/ (Accessed 2/15/16)

Chapman, G. D. (1995). *The Five Love Languages: How to Express Heartfelt Commitment to Your Mate*. Chicago: Northfield Pub.

Corazon, S.S, Stigsdotter, U.K., Moeller, M.S., & Rasmussen, S.M. (2012). Nature as therapist: Integrating permaculture with mindfulness- and acceptance-based therapy in the Danish Healing Forest Garden Nacadia. *European Journal of Psychotherapy and Counseling*, 14(4):335-347.

Csikszentmihalyi, M. (1990). *Flow: The Psychology of Optimal Experience*. New York: Harper & Row.

Curry, K.R., Jaffee, A. (1997). *Nutrition Counseling & Communication Skills*. Philadelphia, PA: WB Saunders Co.

Dalai Lama & Cutler, H. C. (1998). *The Art of Happiness: A Handbook for Living*. New York: Riverhead Books.

Diabetes Prevention Program Research Group (2002). The Diabetes Prevention Program: Description of lifestyle intervention. *Diabetes Care*, 25:2165-2171.

Diener, E., Sandvik, E., et al. (1991). Happiness is the frequency, not the intensity, of positive versus negative affect. In F. Strack, M. Argyle, & N. Schwarz (eds.), Subjective Well-Being: An Interdisciplinary Perspective. 119-139. New York: Pergamon.

Evaro, N., Hackett, L.C., Clark, R.D., Phelan, S. & Hagobian, T.A. (2012). Aerobic exercise reduces neuronal responses in food reward brain regions. *J Appl Physiol.* 112:1612-1619.

Fallon, S. (1999). *Nourishing Traditions*. Washington, D.C.: New Trends Publishing, Inc.

Federal Food, Drug, and Cosmetic Act. URL: http://www.fda.gov/regulatoryinformation/legislation/federalfooddrugandcosmeticactfdcact/ (Accessed 2/21/16)

Food and Nutrition Information Center. "Dietary Reference Intakes: Electrolytes and Water." URL: https://iom.nationalacademies.org/~/media/Files/Activity%20Files/Nutrition/DRIs/DRI_Electrolytes_Water.pdf (Accessed 2/21/16)

Frankl, V. E. (2006). *Man's Search for Meaning*. Boston: Beacon Press.

Fredrickson, B. L. (2013). Updated thinking on positivity ratios. *American Psychologist*, 68(9):814-22.

Ganio, M.S., Armstrong, L.E., Casa, D.J., et al. (2011). Mild dehydration impairs cognitive performance and mood of men. *British Journal of Nutrition*, 106:1535-1543.

Godin, Seth. (2014.) *What to Do When It's Your Turn (and it's Always Your Turn)*. The Domino Project.

Griggs, B. (1997). *Green Pharmacy: The History and Evolution of Western Herbal Medicine*. Rochester, Vt.: Healing Arts Press.

Hasler, C.M. (2002). Functional foods: benefits, concerns and challenges: A position paper from the American Council on Science and Health. *The Journal of Nutrition*, 3772-3781.

Hoffmann, I. (2003). Transcending reductionism in nutrition research. *The American Journal of Clinical Nutrition*, 514S-5516S.

Holmes, O. W. (2012). *Medical Essays, 1842-1882*. Amazon Digital Services, LLC. (Downloaded 2/15/16)

Joireman, J., Shaffer, M.J., et al. (2012). Promotion orientation explains why future-oriented people exercise and eat healthy: Evidence from the two-factor consideration of future consequences-14 Scale. *Personality and Social Psychology Bulletin*, 38:1272.

Jordan, M. & Livingstone, J.B. (2013). Coaching vs. psychotherapy in health and wellness: Overlap, dissimilarities, and the potential for collaboration. *Global Advances in Health & Medicine*, 2(4):20-27.

Kabat-Zinn, J. (1994.) *Wherever You Go, There You Are*. New York: Hyperion.

Katie, B. (2002). *Loving What Is: Four Questions That Can Change Your Life*. New York: Harmony Books.

Katzmarzyk, P. T., Church, T. S., Craig, C. L., & Bouchard, C. (2009). Sitting time and mortality from all causes, cardiovascular disease, and cancer. *Medicine & Science in Sports & Exercise*, 41(5):998–1005.

Kimble, M. (2015). *Unprocessed: My City-Dwelling Year of Reclaiming Real Food*. New York, NY: William Morrow.

King, M. L. (1963). *Strength to Love*. New York: Harper & Row.

Kok, B.E., Waugh, C.E., & Fredrickson, B.L. (2013). Meditation and health: The search for mechanisms of action. *Social and Personality Psychology Compass*, 7(1) 27-39.

Kondō, M., & Hirano, C. (2014). *The Life-Changing Magic of Tidying Up: The Japanese Art of Decluttering and Organizing*. New York: Ten Speed Press.

Lally, P., Van Jaarsveld, C. H. M., Potts, H. W. W. & Wardle, J. (2010). How are habits formed: Modeling habit formation in the real world. *European Journal of Social Psychology*, 40:998-1009.

Lichtenstein, A.H. and Russell, R.M. (2005). Essential nutrients: Food or supplements: Where should the emphasis be? *Journal of the American Medical Association*, 294:351-358.

Liu, R.H. (2003). Health benefits of fruit and vegetables are from additive and synergistic combinations of phytochemicals. *The American Journal of Clinical Nutrition*, 78(3 Suppl):517S-520S.

Livi, S., Alessandri, G., Caprarab, G.V., Pierro, A. (2015). Positivity within teamwork: Cross-level effects of positivity on performance. *Personality and Individual Differences*, 85, 230–235.

Lyubomirsky, S., Sheldon, K.M., & Schkade, D. (2005). Pursuing happiness: The architecture of sustainable change. *Review of General Psychology*, 9, 111-131.

Maslow, A. H. (1954). *Motivation and Personality*. New York: Harper & Row, Publishers.

Matthews, C. E., Chen, K. Y., Freedson, P. S., et al. (2008). Amount of time spent in sedentary behaviors in the United States, 2003-2004. *American Journal of Epidemiology*, 167:875-881.

Maughan, R. J. and Griffin, J. (2003), Caffeine ingestion and fluid balance: a review. *Journal of Human Nutrition and Dietetics*, 16:411–420. doi: 10.1046/j.1365-277X.2003.00477.x (Accessed 2/16/16)

Miller, C. A., & Frisch, M. B. (2009). *Creating Your Best Life: The Ultimate Life List Guide*. New York: Sterling.

Miller, W. R., & Rollnick, S. (2002). *Motivational Interviewing: Preparing People for Change*. New York: Guilford Press.

Miller, W.R. (2009). Ten Things That Motivational Interviewing Is Not. *British Association for Behavioural and Cognitive Psychotherapies*. 37:129-140.

Mollison, B. (1988). *Permaculture: A Designer's Manual*. Australia: Tagari Publications.

National Heart, Lung, and Blood Institute. "How Much Sleep Is Enough?" URL: http://www.nhlbi.nih.gov/health/health-topics/topics/sdd/howmuch (Accessed 2/21/16)

National Weight Control Registry. "NWCR Facts." URL: http://www.nwcr.ws/Research/default.htm (Accessed 2/21/16)

Nestle, M. (2002). *Food Politics*. Berkeley & Los Angeles: University of California Press.

Nutrition and Your Health: Dietary Guidelines for Americans, 2005. 6th ed. Washington, DC: US Government Printing Office.

Office of Disease Prevention and Health Promotion. Dietary Guidelines for Americans 2015-2020 (8th Edition). URL: (Accessed 2/15/16)

Ogden, C. L., Carool, M. D., Kit, B. K., et al. (2014). Prevalence of childhood and adult obesity in the United States. *Journal of the American Medical Association*, 311(8):806-814.

Park, A. "Sitting Is Killing You." *Time Magazine*, Sept. 2, 2014. URL: http://time.com/sitting/ (Accessed 2/21/16)

Pausch, Randy. (2007) *The Last Lecture: Achieving Your Childhood Dreams*. YouTube.com. URL: https://www.youtube.com/watch?v=ji5_MqicxSo (Accessed 2/21/16)

Peale, N. V. (1967). *Enthusiasm Makes the Difference*. Englewood Cliffs, N.J: Prentice-Hall.

Petrini, C. (2003). *Slow Food: The Case for Taste*. New York: Columbia University Press.

Phelps, M. "Everything He Wants to Do is Illegal." *Mother Earth News*, Oct. 1, 2008. URL: http://www.motherearthnews.com/homesteading-and-livestock/sustainable-farming/joel-salatin-interview.aspx?PageId=4#ArticleContent (Accessed 2/15/16)

Popkin, B.M., D'Anci, K.E. & Rosenberg, I.H. (2010). Water, hydration and health. *Nutrition Reviews*, 68(8):439-458.

Position of the Academy of Nutrition and Dietetics (2016). Interventions for the Treatment of Overweight and Obesity in Adults. Journal of the Academy of Nutrition and Dietetics, 116(1):129-147.

Position of the Academy of Nutrition and Dietetics (2013). Functional Foods. Journal of the Academy of Nutrition and Dietetics, 113(8):1096-1103.

Position of the American Dietetic Association (2009). Nutrient Supplementation. Journal of the American Dietetic Association, 109(12):2073–2085.

Prochaska, J., Norcross, J, & DiClemente, C. (2007). *Changing for Good: A Revolutionary Six-Stage Program for Overcoming Bad Habits and Moving Your Life Positively Forward*. New York: HarperCollins.

Ries, E. (2011). *The Lean Startup: How Today's Entrepreneurs Use Continuous Innovation to Create Radically Successful Businesses*. New York: Crown Business.

Rollnick, S., Miller, W. R., & Butler, C. (2008). *Motivational Interviewing in Health Care: Helping Patients Change Behavior*. New York: Guilford Press.

Sandberg, S., & Scovell, N. (2013). *Lean in: Women, Work, and the Will to Lead*. New York: Knopf.

Scientific Report of the 2015 Dietary Guidelines Advisory Committee. URL: http://health.gov/dietaryguidelines/2015-scientific-report/ (Accessed 2/15/16)

Seligman, M., Schulman, P., DeRubeis, R., & Hollon, S. (1999). The prevention of depression and anxiety. *Prevention and Treatment*, 2, article 8. URL: (Accessed 2/16/15)

Seligman, M.P., & Csikszentmihalyi, M. (2000). Positive psychology: an introduction. *American Psychologist*, 55(1):5-14.

Spahn, J.M., Reeves, R.S., Keim, K.S., et al. (2010). State of the evidence regarding behavior change theories and strategies in nutrition counseling to facilitate health and food behavior change. *Journal of the American Dietetic Association*, 110(6):879-891.

Taylor, J.B. (2006). *My Stroke of Insight*. New York: Penguin Group.

Tindle, H.A., Chang, Y., Kuller, L.H., et al. (2009). Optimism, cynical hostility, and incident coronary heart disease and mortality in the Women's Health Initiative. *Circulation*, 120, 656-662.

Tracy, B. (2011). *No Excuses! The Power of Self-Discipline*. Boston: Da Capo Press.

Tribole, E. and Resch, E. (2003). *Intuitive Eating: A Revolutionary Program That Works*. New York: St. Martin's Griffin.

Ungar, M. (2012). Social ecologies and their contribution to resilience. In The Social Ecology of Resilience: A Handbook of Theory and Practice. (pp. 13-31). New York: Springer-Verlag.

USDA's Food and Nutrition Information Center. "How much water should a person drink per day?" URL: http://fnic.nal.usda.gov/how-much-water-should-person-drink-day (Accessed 2/21/16)

Vogliano, C., Brown, K., Miller, A.M., et al. (2015). Plentiful, nutrient-dense food for the world: Guide for Registered Dietitians Nutritionists. *Journal of the Academy of Nutrition and Dietetics*. 115(12) 2014-2018.

Wolever, R.Q., Simmons, L.A., Sforzo, G.A., et al., (2013). A systematic review of the literature on health and wellness coaching: Defining a key behavioral intervention in healthcare. *Global Advances in Health & Medicine*, 2(4):38-57.

Woolf, S. H. (2006). The big answer: rediscovering prevention at a time of crisis in health care. *Harvard Health Policy Review*, 7(2):5-20.

World Health Organization. "WHO Definition of Health." URL: http://www.who.int/trade/glossary/story046/en/ (Accessed 2/21/16)

Yu, Z., Sealey-Potts, C., & Rodriguez, J. (2015). Dietary self-monitoring in weight management: Current evidence on efficacy and adherence. *Journal of the Academy of Nutrition and Dietetics*. 115(12):1931-1938.